16.95

Why Companies Fail

Why Companies Fail

Strategies for Detecting, Avoiding, and Profiting from Bankruptcy

Harlan D. Platt
Northeastern University

Lexington Books
D.C. Heath and Company/Lexington, Massachusetts/Toronto

658.15
P719

Library of Congress Cataloging in Publication Data

Platt, Harlan D.
    Why companies fail.

    Bibliography: p.
    Includes index.
    1. Bankruptcy. I. Title. HG3761.P56   1985   658.1′5   84-48692
ISBN 0-669-09748-9 (alk. paper)
ISBN 0-669-11025-6 (pbk. : alk. paper)

Copyright © 1985 by D.C. Heath and Company

Published simultaneously in Canada
Printed in the United States of America on acid-free paper
Casebound International Standard Book Number: 0-669-09748-9
Paperbound International Standard Book Number: 0-669-11025-6
Library of Congress Catalog Card Number: 84-48692

*To Matthew Platt, my father, and Jerome Bernstein,
my father-in-law*

Contents

Figures

Tables

Preface and Acknowledgments

The stigma once attached to bankruptcy has long since vanished. Both corporations and individuals routinely use Chapter 11 of the current bankruptcy laws, which affords them protection from creditors while they work out a financial reorganization plan. Moreover, innovative uses of bankruptcy are constantly being evolved. For example, Continental Airlines used a Chapter 11 filing to combat a strong labor union, and Manville filed in bankruptcy court because of anticipated liability suits. The future promises even more adaptations by creative managers.

The number of firms filing for bankruptcy court protection as a percentage of all firms has been declining steadily since 1933. One reason for a decline in the failure rate is arguably the increased number of managers with business educations. As a result, fewer firms are failing from sheer incompetence. On the other hand, most business schools ignore the subject of bankruptcy. Students are not trained in how to manage firms that are bankruptcy candidates or that are actually approaching failure. Nor, for that matter, are most business people. *Why Companies Fail* fills this gap. It has been written to highlight the traps that might cause a firm to fail. Examples of failed businesses are employed to increase the reader's understanding of the nature of the pitfalls.

Why Companies Fail describes how to detect firms likely to fail and how to invest in bankrupt companies—how, in short, to gain advantage from bankruptcy. These sections may be most useful to readers in the investments and banking industries, as well as to those who manage their own investments.

As long as technological progress produces new industries and makes older industries obsolete, firms will fail. Until all firms have competent management, sound finances, and outstanding products, firms will fail. My hope is that by educating readers, unnecessary failures can be avoided.

Why Companies Fail is a general book that covers major topics associated with bankruptcy detection, avoidance, and investing. In all cases, readers are advised to seek competent legal, accounting, financial, or other professional advice before taking any actions.

An interest in a subject like bankruptcy must be acquired. In my case, I was intrigued why seemingly healthy firms sometimes failed. Also, I must credit my fortuitous interaction with John Edmunds, a colleague at Northeastern University. John taught me to look for value where others insisted there was none. I hope that someday he finds his lost Dutchman's gold mine in the stacks of Dodge Library.

The *Wall Street Journal*, the *Boston Globe*, the *New York Times*, and *Business Week* were valuable resources in my examination of bankruptcy. I am amazed each day by the number of new failures reported in the financial press. When I began this project, my greatest fear was that I would not be able to uncover enough relevant new cases. Instead I was able to compile extensive lists of potential cases to include.

Several persons provided valuable guidance or assistance in the preparation of this manuscript. Lester Taylor has been a wonderful mentor and friend. I have found many opportunities to utilize his advice. Ron Copeland encouraged me to pursue my interest in bankruptcy and willingly helped me improve the first draft. Coleen Pantalone listened patiently as I endlessly described my new insights. Carol Smith helped gather industry failure data. My editor, Bruce Katz, both encouraged me and noticeably improved the text. Finally, June Remington typed countless versions of the manuscript and never once complained.

In addition, through the years I have benefited from contact and discussions with the following persons: Harold Levinson, Harold Shapiro, Jan Kmenta, Robin Barnes, Jerry Caprio, Marcia McGill, Jim Osten, Otto Eckstein, Jon Welch, John Diffenbach, Dan McCarthy, Phil McDonald, Wes Marple, Lee Atamian, Don Margotta, Ramaswami Murali, David Leggett, Gerald Madden, and Barry Goldberg.

In addition to encouraging me to write, my wife Marjorie's research on banking failures has provided several insights that improved the overall quality of this project. She has been an inspiration as I watch her perform three jobs each day. My daughters, Leah and Sarah, helped me to concentrate and encouraged me to finish. I would also like to thank my mother, Roslyn, who was my original instructor in economics and finance. Had she been born twenty-five years later, I know she would have been a captain of industry. Finally, this book would never have been written had my father not taught me that creating is the most important goal of all.

Why Companies Fail

1
Challenging the Propensity to Fail

I n business there is a thin line between success and failure. Too many companies cross the line and fail. Dun & Bradstreet's 1982 *Business Failure Record* indicates that a business failed every forty-five minutes in 1980, a rate more than 75 percent higher than it had been only two years before. Business failure is not inevitable. A bit of foresight and a moderate amount of common sense can prevent many failures.

Why Companies Fail is written for those who may not be trained in finance or accounting but who need to discover the stumbling blocks responsible for most business failures. Interestingly, although libraries and stores contain countless volumes presenting prescriptions for achieving financial success, almost no attention is focused on avoiding failure. Failure is a topic that, like death, people prefer to ignore. Most individuals' agendas target the illusionary goal of financial independence, despite the fact that only one person in perhaps every one hundred thousand achieves significant wealth. By contrast, each year failure afflicts thousands of people and companies. Perhaps by focusing attention on failure, the number of bankruptcies can be reduced. What follows are simple guidelines that may reduce the likelihood of failure.

The focus of *Why Companies Fail* is business failure. We will identify the critical decisions that may lead a company into bankruptcy, using actual cases of business failure. Because personal financial solvency is affected by many of the same issues, readers may wish to transfer the business guidelines proposed in this book to their personal finances. Companies, after all, are viewed as living entities by the law.

Business failure is remarkably similar to death. The most obvious similarity is that when a company fails, its operations cease; however, unlike natural death, a failed company may be revived. Also, like death, the causes of failure are usually not completely obvious. In some cases, companies do make one overwhelming disastrous decision that leads to a rapid demise, just as when a person fails to look before crossing the street and dies when struck by a garbage truck. Typically, however, a company makes a series of ill-conceived choices that may result from poor management or from the onset of panic following earlier mistakes. Once death or failure occurs, it may be possible in some cases to pinpoint the precise cause of death by conducting an autopsy. In other cases failure occurs for so many reasons that it is not possible to identify a single most important reason for it.

Throughout this book, when a company is classified as having failed because of a particular action or failure to act in a specific way, other mistakes not mentioned in the text will also have contributed to what happened. In fact, different observers might find other errors to have been more important determinants of failure. They may be right. My objective is merely to highlight mistakes companies should avoid.

Readers who find a company's case relevant or interesting can conduct their own in-depth autopsy of its failure by requesting from the company copies of the 10-Q, 10-K, and 8-K reports filed with the Securities and Exchange Commission. 10-Q and 10-K reports are filed each quarter and year, respectively, and discuss the firm's most recent results and future prospects. An 8-K report is filed when a company seeks bankruptcy court protection. Readers who want to follow an ongoing bankruptcy as it works its way through the court system can request copies of the reorganization or liquidation plan and should ask to be placed on the financial mailing list. They can attend shareholders' meetings and should not hesitate to ask questions.

Characterizing Business

I have found it convenient to classify businesses into four categories: eagles, tortoises, condors, and dinosaurs. To determine which animal group to classify a firm into, first judge the quality of its product and then determine its financial condition. Each characteristic, product and financial, is summarized as being healthy or weak. Although most firms deserve intermediate grades between healthy and weak, using extreme characterizations helps me to develop descriptions of why some companies fail and prescriptions of how other firms may avoid bankruptcy. Figure 1–1 uses a matrix to describe the interaction between a business's products and its financial condition. The left side of the matrix refers to financial condition, and the top relates to the product and industry.

Healthy industries produce goods desired by consumers that can be priced at levels that generate profits. Product or industry health refers to both the situation today and how it will change tomorrow. For example, the videotape rental store that just opened in the center of town may appear to have a weak product since sales began slowly; however, the in-

Product and Industry Conditions
Healthy   Weak

	Healthy	Eagle	Tortoise

Financial Condition

Healthy → Eagle | Tortoise

Weak → Condor | Dinosaur

Figure 1–1. Classifying Companies Based on Product and Financial Well-Being

dustry seems healthy considering projections that in a few years, ten times as many homes as today will have videotape players hooked up to television sets. On the other hand, logic tells us that it will be difficult for this particular company to keep out competitors that will begin to appear once profits are being earned. Future profits may not be substantial. How this firm should be classified, as healthy or weak, will depend on an overall assessment. After pulling together all the necessary information, for example, we might conclude that the firm has a healthy product and industry, mostly because it has leased space in an outstanding location.

Financial condition is a more objective measure. It examines financial factors, determining the likelihood that a company will be able to survive into the foreseeable future. A financially weak firm suffers difficulties similar to the anguish of a person with a weak heart. The person's heart might fail at any moment despite the fact that it is now working. Similarly a financially weak firm could fail at any time. The financial condition of most firms is actually intermediate, with part of their finances in good shape and part that are not. *Why Companies Fail* explores the finances of weak firms. So that readers can discover which firms are financially weak, chapter 8 is devoted to failure detection methods.

In assessing a company's financial health, observers must at least consider the following items:

sources of funds

profitability

interest expense

required dividend payments

seasonality of sales

investment in inventory and receivables

leverage conditions

The core chapters in this book examine how these conditions determine a firm's success or failure. Each chapter discusses one potential financial pitfall and illustrates the concept by examining actual company behavior. (Readers should refer to appendix B or the glossary when encountering unfamiliar terms.)

Business people are often better acquainted with product and industry weakness than with financial weakness. To rectify this imbalance, this book focuses on financial problems. Readers are referred to *In Search of Excellence* by Thomas Peters and Robert Waterman, Jr., and *Competitive Strategy* by Michael Porter for interesting ideas in the product and industry areas. Another reason for minimizing the product-industry discussion in this book is that unlike financial difficulties, product problems are more often specific to an industry or situation, and therefore a book built around cases, like this book, would be unduly long.

Product success requires foresight, timing, investment capital, a keen eye for trends, an ability to tailor products to meet (or even create) customer needs, and most of all, a good measure of luck. Consider Thomas Edison. While it is true that he invented the light bulb and other essentials of modern life, his invention of the record player came several decades too soon, and it languished unused. In this case, Edison lacked the timing necessary for success.

The free enterprise system, the backbone of U.S. capitalism, rewards success but punishes failure. Fortunately the system is myopic. If not, Dr. An Wang whose firm, Wang Computer, was at one time struggling, would not today be called by *Forbes* one of the five richest Americans.

Four types of enterprises are identified by combining the product and financial characteristics of companies, as depicted in figure 1–1. Probably the greatest difference between the four types of firms is their prospects for the future:

Eagles will prosper.

Condors have a tendency to survive.

Tortoises will endure mundane survival.

Dinosaurs are guaranteed failure.

No firm's outlook is permanent or guaranteed. A single mistake or miscalculation can transform even an eagle into a dinosaur. Thus, each of the cases presented in this book to illustrate failure traps is preceded by a diagram showing a healthy animal being transformed into a dinosaur.

Eagles soar. Eagles have healthy products and strong finances. A company like IBM, a leader in product development in a growing industry with overwhelming financial backing, is the best example of an eagle. Future prosperity is virtually guaranteed for IBM. Either the company will independently develop new products to ensure sales growth, or it will rely on its financial strength to enter markets developed by others once technological uncertainties and market potentials are resolved. The financial pitfalls that await firms with fewer resources do not pose a challenge to an eagle.

At the opposite extreme are dinosaurs. For the dinosaur, the future is bleak. Companies in this, the worst category, not only have trouble selling their product but lack the financial support required to develop new products or markets. Consider W.T. Grant's plight. Grant's tried to compete with well-managed firms like Sears and K-Mart but lacked adequate finances to be on an equal footing with them. When product problems surfaced, the financial well was not deep enough to save Grant's. Like a dinosaur, it failed and vanished.

Companies are not born dinosaurs. Reputable businesses are not formed to sell worthless products, nor are companies created in a financially hopeless condition. Companies must follow a special path to become a dinosaur. First, managers must ignore market trends and allow the firm's products to become either obsolete or overpriced. Second, the company's financial condition must be allowed to deteriorate as a cascade of financial crises culminates in a quagmire of indecision and external decision making.

Each of the two remaining categories of business firms, tortoises and condors, possesses one strong and one weak characteristic. A tortoise is a firm that is financially healthy but is competing in a troubled industry or whose product is encountering market resistance. An example of a tortoise might be Chock-Full-o'-Nuts. This low-debt, rich-in-assets company sells coffee in a market where its competitors have enormous advertising budgets. Chock-Full-o'-Nuts has a questionable future despite the premium quality of its coffee. But because it has few creditors and untold millions in undervalued real estate assets, mostly located in New York City, Chock-Full-o'-Nuts' survival is not threatened. It could go on forever. Still, new management is taking steps to improve the firm's future by focusing on new product development.

Condors, like dinosaurs, are not designed for the twentieth century, but unlike the dinosaur, the great condor has somehow managed to survive. Condors may become extinct at any time. Their survival hinges on maintaining a delicate balance among hostile forces. Some companies are condors too. These firms have survived to the present but lack the financial fortitude to weather many more storms. They could fail at anytime. I prefer not to identify specific examples of business condors since to do so might bring harm to an innocent company. Instead, readers are referred to chapter 8, where bankruptcy detection methods are explained to enable readers to identify condors.

Of the two principal causes of business failure, product or financial difficulties, this book addresses only financial issues. Product or industry problems are often unique to the company, its location, or its managers and thus are better resolved on an individual company basis. Although the examples in this book are from relatively mature companies, the lessons are applicable to start-up businesses as well.

Condors and dinosaurs are the main subject of this book: dinosaurs because they constitute the population of known business failures, condors because these are the companies we can hope to save. Examination of dinosaurs can help to identify decisions that in the past have sent companies into oblivion. Condors are provided with self-examination methods that help identify the need to change if failure is to be averted.

Characterizing Failure

Business failure assumes many forms. At the extremes are total failures ending in bankruptcy and simple economic failures that may remain in business for a long time. A listing of business failures in order of increasing severity is given in table 1–1. Bankruptcy appears at the bottom of the list. When bankrupt, a firm is dead; all that remains is for creditors to hear the last will and testament, known as the liquidation report.

Table 1–1
Categories of Business Failure

Economic Failure

    Step 1: Opportunity losses: Earnings are minimal

    Step 2: Negative profits: The company is losing money

Financial Failure

    Step 1: Technical insolvence: Current obligations cannot be met

    Step 2: Bankruptcy: The company has no real net worth

Note: Listed in order of increasing severity.

Economic, as distinct from financial, failure occurs when the business is not sufficiently prosperous given the level of capital investment and human effort put into making it work. Look at it this way: entrepreneurs have an opportunity value, which is how much they could earn if they were employed by another company. Similarly, monies invested in a firm could be redeployed to other investments and there earn financial rewards. Thus, a firm that is earning a profit may still be an economic failure if the earnings are not sufficient reward given the level of human and other resources being devoted to the business. A good example of this type of economic failure is the corner gas station that for survival requires the owner to work seventy-two hours per week. For all intents and purposes, the owner in deciding to keep the station open, is valuing his or her own time as being worth about $1.25 an hour. The owner has decided not to get an outside job at a higher rate of pay and chooses to undervalue his or her own labor resource. This is the least severe form of economic failure since the firm survives as long as the owner is willing to earn less than his or her opportunity value.

Banks and other lending institutions never volunteer to reduce interest charges to firms that are economic failures. Rather, the owner must in essence subsidize the banks by taking even less for himself or herself. If no outside funds are involved in the business, the owner must understand that personal capital too has an opportunity value, just like entrepreneurial time. In the case of the gas station, the owner might be able to net out $20,000 by selling the business back to the oil company. An investment in a money market fund might annually generate $2,000 or more on a $20,000 investment. The scale of the economic failure is thus even greater in the case of a business using only internal funds if the entrepreneur fails to deduct the opportunity value of the invested money.

Economic failure on a grand scale occurs when the business loses money. The cash drain can continue as long as the owners continue to contribute capital. Eventually, though, the business probably becomes a financial failure. Then a remedy is sought. In some cases, economic failures turn around on their own as business improves. For example, many of the new genetics research companies are not only losing money but as of this writing have few real products to sell. If company research leads to marketable products—for example, a cure for a dread disease—the situation will immediately reverse itself. Otherwise the companies must eventually become a financial failure.

There are two types of financial failure: technical insolvency and bankruptcy. The technically insolvent firm has assets with real value in excess of its liabilities—the owners in theory should be able to walk away with some cash after paying off debts if the firm were to be liquidated—but it is unable to meet all its current financial obligations. These obligations may be repayment of a short-term loan, payments to suppliers, or even repayment of the current portion of its long-term debt. Creditors need to be placated if the firm is to avoid reorganization. Often technically insolvent firms are capable of surviving and prospering for a long time if they can overcome the near-term liquidity crises. At one time Chrysler was near to being technically insolvent. Now Chrysler is reporting record profits. In other cases, however (such as Charter, which filed for Chapter 11 bankruptcy in April 1984), the technically insolvent firm is unable to satisfy creditors' demands and must seek court protection. The withdrawal of further credit often halts the ability of this type of firm to continue operating.

Bankruptcy is the ultimate financial failure. Here the firm is found to have a lower real asset value than is necessary to pay off all its liabilities. In other words, more money is owed than could ever be repaid. Bankrupt firms do not always die. In some cases, the firm is viewed as worth more alive than dead, and the company is reorganized rather than liquidated. Recently, for example, Wickes reported that as a result of reorganizing, its creditors will receive $400 million to $500 million more than if the company had been liquidated (some $450 million). Some bankrupt firms are considered better off dead. For example, W.T. Grant, which went bankrupt in 1975, was liquidated with all of its assets sold to pay off its creditors. Sometimes in a liquidation or a reorganization, creditors receive $0.20 on the dollar or less.

An interesting example of how to use the word *real* in the discussion of assets and bankruptcy is found by examining Texas International (TEI). In 1984, this oil exploration company announced that as a result of new engineering estimates and a change in accounting methods, it was lowering the value of its book assets (mostly land and oil) by $270 million. TEI's before and after 1983 balance sheet is given in table 1–2. After the announcement, the firm's reported net worth was negative $95.4 million, implying that the common stock traded on the New York Stock Exchange was valueless. However, immediately after the announcement, the stock traded at between $2 and $3 per share, and the company did not declare bankruptcy. One month after the announcement, TEI's bankers increased its credit line (the borrowable funds available to the company).

How could a firm with a negative net worth, like TEI, continue to operate? The key to the riddle is the concept of real net worth, which evaluates assets at market prices or at what-they-would-fetch values. A TEI report stated that its economically recoverable reserves of oil and gas were valued at slightly more than its total liabilities, and thus its real net worth is larger than the reported value in table 1–2 and is positive.

Table 1–2
Texas International's 1983 Balance Sheet
(millions of dollars)

	Before			After		
	Assets	*Liabilities and Net Worth*		*Assets*	*Liabilities and Net Worth*	
Current assets	$ 67.2	Liabilities	$438.6	Current assets	$ 67.2	Liabilities	$438.6
Long-term assets	546.0	Net worth	174.6	Long-term assets	276.0	Net worth	(95.4)
Total	613.2		613.2		343.2		343.2

U.S. business is summarized by two words: *risk* and *return*. Risk denotes the likelihood of failure; return describes profitability. A maxim of modern financial theory is that higher risk should be taken only when it is compensated by higher return. A great deal of time and energy on Wall Street is spent looking for investments with greater returns than other investments with the same amount of risk. For example, the microcomputer business is an environment promising great riches, but it also holds great risk. Not too surprisingly, a number of minicomputer makers have failed in the past few years. One may conclude that surviving firms will be profitable.

The Route away from Failure

Once a firm is a financial failure (see table 1–1), a remedy must be found to keep creditors at bay, or else creditors will file in the bankruptcy courts an involuntary petition of bankruptcy. Technically insolvent firms attempt either to extend or compose their debt. Extension delays interest and principal payments to give the firm time to overcome its short-term difficulties. Extension requests are sometimes made by companies not yet insolvent but anticipating such an eventuality. Lenders are more likely to respond favorably to a request for extension made in advance since it demonstrates that financial matters are not out of control. Normally all debt will be extended for an equal period of time. Thus all creditors contribute equally to the revitalization scheme. It is possible, however, that a disproportionately small lender may be able to exact continued interest and principal payments with the acquiescence of other lenders who prefer to extend their debt for a short period of time rather than push the firm into formal and costly bankruptcy proceedings.

A situation akin to this developed when International Harvester proposed a debt restructuring plan to its lenders. Several small banks with relatively insignificant proportions of International Harvester's debt adopted a squeaky wheel policy, refusing to give in to the company's demands.

Composition of debt involves lenders' voluntarily reducing the principal amount of the debt. The objective of composition is to lower permanently the firm's annual interest or fixed charge requirements. Composition is designed to spawn a new environment in which costs are easier to cover since there is less interest to pay and profits are more easily earned. Lenders do not compose debt gratuitously. In exchange for composing debt, lenders often receive shares of stock or warrants to purchase shares at reduced prices. For example, in the International Harvester debt restructuring plan proposed December 15, 1983, $1 billion in debt would be converted into 70 million common stock shares, controlling about 63 percent of the company. In effect, composition converts debt into ownership. Composition is not an advantageous way to sell stock. Like a fire sale, damaged goods are being sold by composition. Hence the firm must discount the price of its stock below what it would sell for if there were no difficulties.

Frequently composition and extension occur simultaneously. For example, when a firm fails to make an interest payment or to cover a preferred stock dividend, it has begun to extend its debt. Immediately creditors are contacted, meetings are arranged, and a composition plan is proposed. All the while extension is occurring. Finally, a plan of composition is agreed on and debt repayment begins, or else the firm moves to the next step and enters the bankruptcy court either voluntarily or involuntarily.

The bankrupt firm, one whose real net worth is exceeded by its accumulated liabilities, has two choices: liquidate or reorganize. (Strategies for the near bankrupt are given in chapter 9.) In liquidation, a firm's assets are sold to the highest bidder, and the proceeds are distributed to creditors according to a specific plan. When a firm is reorganized, the creditors, shareholders, and representatives of the court come together and perform the miracle of rebirth. A company that has died is refashioned with improved financial and product characteristics and is reincarnated. The objective is to convert the dinosaur into an eagle. Of course, given the material with which they have to work, eagles often cannot be created. Something less, possibly a condor or a tortoise, is likely to rise from the ashes.

It is possible to create an eagle out of a dinosaur, though. Take the case of Toys-R-Us. After being refashioned by the courts and the committees of creditors and owners, the firm emerged from bankruptcy as the dominant seller of toys in the Western world, selling almost 10 percent of all toys. Investors who paid $1 per share for Toys-R-Us immediately after it emerged from bankruptcy today have stock worth in excess of $50 per share (see chapter 10). Success stories like this one are atypical. Many reorganized companies fail a second time. for example, HRT Industries, which is now in Chapter 11 bankruptcy proceedings, had been in Chapter 11 just nine years ago.

A general comparison of key aspects of each route out of failure is given in table 1–3. Probably the most important difference among the four methods is that only in liquidation does the firm cease to exist. After extension, composition, and reorganization, the firm reemerges as a solvent enterprise. The longevity of this enterprise is, however, another matter. Liquidation is a solution of last resort since the firm's assets are often sold for less than their true worth in a liquidation sale. It is also true, however, that in an attempt to raise capital and lower debts, assets may be sold at deep discounts whenever a firm is in financial trouble.

The issuance of new common shares is commonly part of any plan for a firm to emerge from financial difficulties. In some cases, the shares are exchanged for debt to create more equity capital and to reduce fixed-charge obligations. In other situations, new common stock warrants (long-term stock options) may be sold to investors. Even when debt instruments are sold by a troubled company, frequently conversion rights

Table 1–3
Outcomes of Financial Failure

	Extension	Composition	Liquidation	Reorganization
Does the firm survive?	Yes	Yes	No	Yes
Do debt levels get reduced?	No	Yes	Yes	Yes
Do repayment delays occur?	Yes	No	No	Yes
Do all creditors suffer equally?	Yes	No	No	No
Do bankruptcy courts participate?	No	No	Yes	Yes
Do more common shares frequently get issued?	No	Yes	No	Yes
Do the firm's assets often sell at less than true value?	No	No	Yes	No
Do parts of the company get sold to raise money?	Yes	Yes	No	Yes

Table 1–4
Priority of Bankruptcy Claims

1. Costs associated with the bankruptcy, such as legal fees
2. Certain wages owed employees
3. Taxes owed
4. Secured creditors
5. Unsecured creditors
6. Preferred stockholders
7. Common stockholders

are attached to the debt to allow the new lenders to convert the debt into stock and thereby participate fully in the company's recovery.

Creditors are not viewed as equals when a firm fails. Senior creditors are compensated before subordinated creditors, who are compensated before stockholders. Table 1–4 provides a simplified listing of the priority schedule for bankruptcy claims. Since common stockholders are last on the list, their claims may not be repaid.

The next six chapters highlight the types of financial predicaments that may befall any company. Companies will arguably stand a better chance of avoiding failure if these chapters enable them to acquire better financial practices. Unlike companies that fail, surviving companies need not absorb the complicated legal and accounting ramifications of bankruptcy. In the event that the next six chapters keep a company from failing, that firm's emotional and financial savings will exceed by many times the costs of implementing the new ideas.

2
Financial Reasons for Failure

Other books teach managers how to achieve success. This book presents a different focus: what actions will cause businesses to go bankrupt. (In this chapter and throughout the rest of this book, unless otherwise stated, the word *bankruptcy* will mean business failure, technical insolvency, and voluntary and involuntary bankruptcy. The distinctions among these categories of failure are less important in a financial book than in a legal or accounting text.) The biggest difference between the two approaches is that precise rules can be articulated when success is the focus. When the topic is bankruptcy, rules are replaced by reason. The need to use reason instead of rules is demonstrated by considering what would happen if either a success rule or a bankruptcy rule were violated. When a success rule is not followed, at worst a lower profit is earned. Making a business profit is like winning at the racetrack. As long as your horse wins, you can accept any margin of victory. In horse racing and business, winning is everything.

Now consider what might occur if there existed a list of rules for avoiding bankruptcy. First, armed with such a list, dissident shareholders might unjustifiably accuse well-run companies of poor management. In addition, unnecessary bankruptcies might occur if managers became sanguine after checking and double-checking that none of the rules is violated. The trouble lies in the exception that proves the rule, and in the case of bankruptcy, the consequence is too costly.

The strategy adopted in this book is to isolate the basic business precepts that firms must consciously seek adherence to. While violation of any one precept may not of itself lead to failure, each precept can in a given situation be a time bomb waiting to explode. Instead of giving rules to follow, my intention is to enable readers to feel the storm before it arrives. The objective is perception and not regimentation. For that reason, actual cases of business failure are presented in chapters 3 through 7. Instead of a total understanding, readers should endeavor to perceive how errors were made. Chapter 8 discusses bankruptcy detection methods, and chapter 9 is devoted to strategies for the near bankrupt. Readers may wish to develop rules for their own firms after reading chapters 8 and 9.

Using perception works best if the senses are overly strong. At worst, a too-strong method will occasionally detect an about-to-happen bankruptcy that is only imaginary. In exchange, a too-strong method rarely fails to detect a real upcoming bankruptcy. I would speculate that when asked to choose between an approach that is too sensitive or one that is not sensitive enough, most business managers would opt for the former. This feeling is premised on the fact that failure exacts a high price, while fear of failure promotes improvement.

The next five chapters articulate precise financial reasons for bankruptcy. Each chapter refers to one of the following problems: the cash-flow cycle, current assets, operating leverage, financial leverage, and debt maturity. Bankruptcy may result from difficulties caused by any or all of these topics.

The *cash-flow cycle* concerns the relationship between when revenues are received and when expenses are paid. Revenues and expenses are not usually synchronously matched. The asynchronicity creates the potential for a cash-flow cycle problem that could culminate in bankruptcy.

Firms must strive to keep an acceptable balance of *current assets*, by which I mean cash, inventory, accounts receivable, and other short-term assets. Bankruptcies resulting from an imbalance in current assets may be the most easily avoided since what is required is that managers monitor and adjust the levels of each current asset.

Operating leverage concerns a firm's fixed (unavoidable) cost relative to the profits it can earn from additional sales. Firms consider alternative operating leverage levels as part of their strategic plans as they compare various acquisitions of machines and equipment. While machines tend to lower average costs, they also tend to raise the number of units of product that must be sold to break even. Bankruptcy may result if too many machines are acquired.

Financial leverage reports on the impact on net income of the firm's choice of financing. The two basic choices are to finance with debt (borrowed money) or equity (money raised from the owners). Some aggressive entrepreneurs prefer to finance with as much debt as possible since ownership is thereby restricted. The disadvantage to this approach is that debt holders require periodic interest payments (which raises costs) and the eventual return of their funds (which imposes a refinancing problem). With equity funds, on the other hand, annual interest payments are lower. If, however, a large number of common shares must be sold in order to raise the equity capital needed, it becomes more difficult to report sizable per share earnings or to have the common stock price rise.

The choice between using debt or stock is important since it affects both the firm's likelihood of bankruptcy and its potential future earnings.

The final bankruptcy issue, *debt maturity*, concerns a firm's decision to borrow money in either the short or long term. The perfect example of this in our personal lives is the decision to buy a home with a fixed rate mortgage or to take the chance that interest rates will not rise and use a variable rate mortgage. If interest rates stay the same or fall, the variable mortgage provides a lower cost of home ownership; however, if interest rates rise, monthly payments rise with a variable mortgage, and people not able to make the higher payments lose their homes. Companies also gamble on interest rate changes. Sometimes they win, and they report higher profits; sometimes they lose and go bankrupt.

It is easy to moralize and say that businesses should not engage in interest rate gambles since firms are established to manufacture products or sell services and not to gamble. It might also seem legitimate to require companies to borrow only money with fixed rates of interest. But the adoption of a policy reducing the manager's prerogative on financing the enterprise makes as little sense as would a policy requiring a firm always to have a certain amount of inventory or never to extend credit to its customers. When managers think interest rates are high and nearing peak levels, they do not want to lock themselves into a long-term commitment. If the manager is wrong and rates rise further, failure may result. But this failure is balanced by countless other successes, when money is saved as interest rates fall.

Appendix A points out the large number of business failures in the United States and how this number has been increasing over the past several years. If the title of this book had been *Why Companies Succeed,* the appendix would have discussed the number of multibillion dollar enterprises or the number of new multimillionaires in the United States. In other words, success balances failure, and the freedom to choose is what ultimately permits both. If managers are legislated from taking risks, they will also be prohibited from achieving success.

3
Getting Caught in the Cash-Flow Cycle

I t's easy to get rich in business. Just make a product, sell it, and bring your money to the bank." If it were that simple, almost all of us would be rich. These statements are not false, just naive, ignoring the complexity of business and business operations.

One important, though frequently ignored, business concept is something I have called the *time factor*. The time factor counts the number of days between a decision to produce a product and when money is actually received from selling the good. The time factor quantifies the cash-flow cycle. During the cash-flow cycle, the firm's bank account fluctuates from a deficit to a surplus level. The deficit does not indicate a weak financial position but shows only that the firm is waiting to get paid for its services. If, however, preparations are not made to cover the deficit, the firm's finances are not only weak, but the business cannot exist for long. Moreover, if the deficit is larger than expected or if lenders doubt that the deficit will ever become a surplus, credit may be withdrawn, and the firm will fail.

Table 3–1 illustrates a typical cash-flow cycle. The cycle starts when materials (workers, office space, raw materials, and so on) are purchased. The purchase leads to the simultaneous creation of an accounts payable and of inventory. In the next step, the inventory is turned into finished goods, which are sold to consumers. The sale is made on credit, so an accounts receivable is registered. Finally, the receivable is collected, and the firm receives funds. The number of days elapsing between events in the figure represent what is experienced by a typical business. The time factor equals the thirty days from when the firm pays money out, on the tenth day, until money is received, on the fortieth day. Usually a bank credit line is established to finance the time factor. Lines of credit run not just for thirty days but for an entire year since if production continues, the cash-flow cycle repeats over and over again.

Managerial actions may change the time factor; that is, the time factor is variable depending on a series of choices concerning the extension

Table 3–1
Typical Cash-Flow Cycle

Day	Activity	Cash In (+) or Out (−)
1	Purchase raw material; create an account payable	No cash
2–10	Put material into inventory and begin production	No cash
10	Pay for material	−
10	Sell product; create an account receivable	No cash
40	Collect receivable	+
Time Factor = 40 (money in) − (money out) = 30		

of credit, the taking of trade discounts, the nature of the production process, and the offering of trade discounts. How each of these decisions affects the cash-flow cycle is shown in table 3–2. For example, if a firm chooses to relax its credit terms, its time factor grows since fewer cash sales are made. The secondary impacts are even more important: sales and bad debts both rise. While profits will rise if sales increase, higher bad debt losses can cause profits to fall. The time factor will also rise if a firm begins taking trade discounts that require early payment. Moreover, the time factor can be lowered by shortening the production process or offering discounts to customers for early payment.

Table 3–2
Changing Cash Flows with Four Managerial Choices

Action	Impact on Time Factor	Further Effects
More lenient credit terms (allow more customers to use credit)	Increase	Sales rise, more bad debts
Take more trade discounts (pay bills sooner)	Increase	Higher profits if trade discount is worth more than the cost of finance
Simplify production process (reduce production steps)	Decrease	May increase financing requirement if new facilities must be purchased
Offer trade discounts (cut price to cash customers)	Decrease	Profits may fall, bad debts reduced

Companies with access to sufficient financing may choose to lengthen their time factor. This action would lead to an increase in the amount of funds they must borrow. The decision would be based on whether these actions lead to higher profits. For example, a firm might start to pay for its purchases within ten days because its suppliers are offering 2 percent cash discounts for customers not taking the usual thirty days to pay. Taking cash discounts can be very profitable. The rate of return earned by a firm paying in ten days and taking a 2 percent cash discount is 37 percent. If the firm can borrow money at less than 37 percent interest, taking the discount is profitable. Thus, the firm's profits rise when it takes more trade discounts and increases the time factor.

Presumably profits are made on each sale. Some of these profits could be used to reduce steadily the company's debt. Eventually the firm might have enough cash to finance the time factor itself. Most firms choose not to be conservative and do not finance the cash-flow cycle themselves. Instead profits generated from product sales are reinvested in new production facilities or are spent diversifying into new markets. Thus the continued extension of credit by lending institutions to firms is an essential and necessary part of doing business. It also constitutes a potential bankruptcy trap.

The uneven balance in the teeter-totter contest between the eagle and the dinosaur depicted in figure 3–1 shows the importance of banks to a firm confronting a cash-flow cycle. As long as banks are willing to lend money, the fulcrum beneath the cash-flow cycle is close enough to the dinosaur to permit the eagle to maintain an equilibrium with the dinosaur. That is, an uneven pattern of cash receipts and disbursements (the cash-flow cycle) is permitted by the activities of lenders. Were the

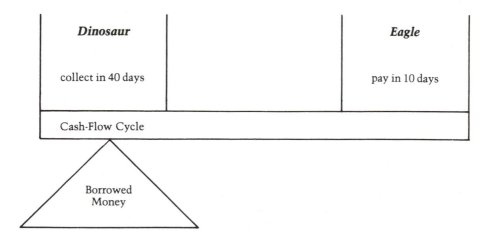

Figure 3–1. Balancing the Cash-Flow Cycle

bank to withdraw its credit, the fulcrum would shift toward the center, the eagle would be tossed off the teeter-totter, and the firm would be bankrupt, a dinosaur.

Banks and other lending institutions are not the only sources of funds to cover a cash-flow cycle. In weak industries, suppliers may be forced to lengthen their payment period so that the time factor is cut to zero days. An example of this are house and garden shops, which purchase chemical fertilizers, seeds, and other products from major chemical companies. Without supplier credit, purchases would be reduced, if not stopped altogether.

Other companies, not wanting to be at the mercy of a bank, maintain cash reserves sufficient to carry them over the peak of the cash-flow cycle. This type of conservative financial practice has some advantages. Unlike bank borrowers, these firms need not entirely pay off their loan once a year. Banks usually insist on having credit lines reduced to a zero balance once a year as a means to certify the borrower's financial health. This practice is similar to credit card companies' asking cardholders to pay off their debt when a credit limit has been reached before increasing the limit. Critics of this practice contend that a higher limit is needed when you reach the limit, but the banks need to be convinced that the cardholder deserves more credit.

Charter   Eagle ⟶ Dinosaur

Charter was an archetypical U.S. success story. On the financial side, net income of $0.94 per share in 1977 catapulted to earnings of $14.93 per share in 1979. On $4 billion of revenue in 1979, the company earned an impressive $365 million in net income. The stock price reacted to the company's good fortune and jumped from about $3.00 per share in 1977 to nearly $50.00 a share in 1979. With 20 million outstanding common shares, Charter's market value went from about $60 million in 1977 to almost $1 billion in 1979.

For a company that began as a family-owned lumber yard and then grew into being the owner of several major publications, including the *Ladies Home Journal*, insurance subsidiaries, and several mammoth oil refineries, the next five years, 1979–1984, were not as pleasant. Although revenues reached $5.6 billion in 1983, the company's finances began to weaken. In April 1984, the company and 43 of its 183 subsidiaries filed for protection from its creditors under Chapter 11 of the bankruptcy code.

The tale of this bankruptcy is told in two parts. The first relates how problems began. The second describes how the cash-flow cycle eventually led to the company's demise.

The title to Charter's first tale could be "Those Who Live by the Sword, Die by the Sword." It begins with Charter's earning enormous profits from its refinery operations. These profits fueled an expansion and diversification drive. Refinery profits existed because of favorable contracts with oil-producing countries like Libya. Charter bought crude oil cheaply, processed it, and sold high-margin refined products. Beginning in 1980, the market for refined oil products weakened, as did the market for crude oil. But refined oil product prices fell by more than crude oil prices, in part because major oil companies own both refineries and oil fields. As a result, Charter was paying more for its raw materials than it was receiving for its finished product, residual fuel. Even high-volume sales could not compensate. Losses accumulated, and the firm's cash drained away.

At this point, story 2 begins. The title of this story might be "It Sometimes Pays to Bite the Bullet." When the troubles began, Charter became even more aggressive. First, it traded a valuable asset (8 percent of the stock of St. Joseph Paper Company) for 18 percent of its own shares. In effect, this action converted a valuable, salable asset into a potentially unsalable asset. Common stock buy-back plans usually emanate from companies with excess cash. Then Charter invested $123 million in another expansion. Creditors were baffled by these actions. They would have preferred more conservative, cautionary strategy. First, the company might have written down the value shown on the balance sheet of its refinery to reflect the realities of the oil market. Second, it might have attempted to conserve, not spend, cash. Creditors finally took action. Charter was informed by its creditors, in this case crude oil suppliers, that it would no longer be allowed to buy oil on credit; the ten-day grace period provided by accounts payable financing vanished. The fulcrum in figure 3–1 shifted abruptly to the right. Without trade credit, Charter was a dinosaur. Almost immediately, it filed for protection in the bankruptcy court.

Lionel   Condor ⟶ Dinosaur

The cash-flow cycle is aggravated if a company's business is seasonal. In a seasonal business, sales are not evenly distributed across the year. One season or one quarter may have significantly greater sales activity than the rest of the year. Seasonal businesses frequently earn all or most of their profits during a peak season. During the rest of the year, they may break even or even lose money. Examples of seasonal businesses are vacation resorts, bicycle manufacturers, and snow plow manufacturing and sales.

Lionel, a Pennsylvania-based toy retailer, engages in one of the most highly seasonal businesses of all: the sale of toys. Almost 50 percent of Lionel's yearly sales occur in the fourth quarter of the year versus just 15 percent of sales that occur in the first quarter. Given the fixed costs that must be covered throughout the year, it would be difficult for Lionel not to lose money in the first quarter. Suppose that Lionel broke even in the fourth quarter; that is, total revenues equaled total cost during the three months of the fourth quarter of the year. Lionel would have to reduce costs by 70 percent to stay at break-even in the first quarter since first-quarter revenues equal just 30 percent of fourth-quarter revenue.

During slow periods, firms in seasonal businesses try to control costs and limit their losses. However, some costs (such as rent, interest payments, and managerial and executive salaries) are not reducible; these fixed costs must be paid unless the firm purposefully reduces the scale of its operation by subleasing space or laying off permanent workers.

Lionel's fixed costs were substantial. Unsecured general creditors (creditors whose debt is not guaranteed by specified assets), mostly toy manufacturers, were owed in excess of $100 million, and in addition there were $15 million in bonds outstanding receiving 10 5/8 percent interest. Lionel was operating over 100 toy stores with sizable fixed operating expenses: salaries, utilities, rents, and lease payments. Lionel regularly lost money during off-quarters.

Figure 3–2 illustrates how profits vacillate with sales in a seasonal business like Lionel's. As long as fourth-quarter profits outweighed losses from the first three quarters, Lionel reported an annual profit. As long as the banks had confidence in management's abilities to operate the company properly, credit was extended to cover the normal cash-flow cycle and to provide enough credit to carry the firm into the fourth quarter.

The bells tolled for Lionel in 1982. Bankers lost confidence in management's abilities, and the money-losing quarters were approaching. The bankers had to choose between two strategies:

1. Maintain the credit line (the maximum extendable loan), knowing that losses would be incurred for six to nine months and then hope that the management team could pull off a good quarter.
2. Cancel the credit line and limit its losses.

The bankers chose the second alternative. Without the credit line, Lionel could not purchase toys and other supplies for the upcoming season. It became a dinosaur and was forced to seek Chapter 11 bankruptcy protection from its creditors.

There are two possible outcomes after a company files for Chapter 11 bankruptcy: reorganization or liquidation. In *reorganization*, the

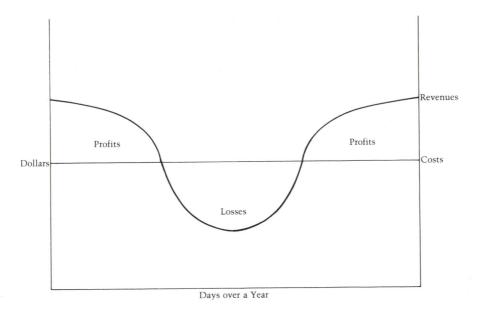

Figure 3–2. Profits and Losses for a Seasonal Business

firm's operations and finances are refashioned, and a healthy organization replaces one that was unable to meet its obligations. *Liquidation* occurs when all assets are converted into cash and the proceeds are used at least to fulfill partially the firm's existing indebtedness. Reorganization is always preferred to liquidation, though sometimes reorganizing is not possible. The basic question that decides the better route to follow is whether the firm's assets are worth more in reorganization or in liquidation. That is, is the company worth more dead than alive? Lionel was reorganized.

The members of the company's board of directors understood the need for a good relationship with lenders. Almost immediately after filing the Chapter 11 petition, a new management team was brought in. This action gave creditors confidence that the firm could be salvaged. Different banks provided a new credit line. These new debts assumed a bankruptcy priority above the old debt. Thus, the new bankers are virtually assured of repayment. The company is expected to emerge from bankruptcy in 1985.

The first step taken by the new managers of Lionel was to stem the losses that were draining resources. They outlined a plan to "reduce costs, eliminate non-essential corporate overhead and restructure the business while improving productivity and profitability."[1] This plan was probably effected by a careful analysis of each of the 105 toy stores.

Each store's contribution to profits and to corporate overhead expense would be determined, and nonperforming stores would be shut down. Lionel rapidly slimmed down to 53 toy stores in 14 states. New accounting controls, marketing techniques, and operating methods were introduced so that each of the remaining stores could reach its full potential.

In correcting a failing company's faults, managers focus on both cost-reduction and revenue-bolstering methods. Profits, after all, are the difference between revenues and costs, and this strategy therefore produces the maximum possible profit. It is vital to note, however, that while in Chapter 11 bankruptcy, firms do not pay finance charges, so that reported profits or losses are not reflecting all charges. If a recovery strategy is working, revenues should grow, and costs should be reduced while the firm is working out a plan of reorganization. Lionel's postbankruptcy filing quarterly reports are summarized in table 3–3. The table shows that Lionel's new managers have succeeded in turning the firm around. Profitability has been regained. A reorganized Lionel would thus stand a good chance of never again needing to be protected from its creditors. The courts would refer to this as a "feasible" reorganization.

Part of the reason for Lionel's return to profitability is due to the fact that the company owns 82 percent of Dale Electronics, Inc., a manufacturer of electronic components. The strong economic recovery experienced in the United States during 1983–1984 contributed to substantial growth in the demand for Dale's products. In fact, during the first quarter of 1984, Dale's profits that were reported by Lionel (companies may consolidate financial reports when they own more than 80 percent of the stock in another company) equaled approximately $3.1 million. Since Lionel reported only a $1.0 million total profit in this quarter, the toy stores actually lost about $2 million during this slow toy selling quarter.

The second important reorganization criterion evaluated by the bankruptcy court before approving a proposed plan of reorganization is termed "fairness" and refers to the issue of whether all creditors and stockholders are treated fairly and equitably given the seniority of their claim. If the plan is fair and feasible, it will be approved.

Lionel has three major classes of creditors: general unsecured creditors who were owed approximately $100 million, holders of a subordinated debenture (a bond with a low repayment priority) who were owed $15 million, and the current holders of the approximately 7.1 million outstanding shares of common stock. Its principal assets were some cash, the toy business, and its 82 percent holdings in Dale Electronics. It became obvious almost immediately that the Dale stock would need to be sold in order to raise cash to repay the creditors. What was not known was how valuable Dale Electronics really was.

Table 3–3
Lionel's Quarterly Income Statement since Filing Chapter 11
(millions of dollars)

	1982	1983				1984	
	4th Quarter	1st Quarter	2nd Quarter	3rd Quarter	4th Quarter	1st Quarter	2nd Quarter
Revenues	$140.7	$39.8	$53.4	$55.9	$146.7	$59.6	$74.2
Costs	148.9	44.3	54.5	59.1	144.7	59.1	72.4
Net profit (loss)[a]	(8.2)	(4.5)	(1.1)	(3.2)	2.0	1.0	1.8

Note: Lionel owns 82 percent of Dale Electronics, an electronics component manufacturer. The company reports consolidated results for the toy and electronics firm.
[a]Net profit may include returned federal taxes because of the company's ability to write off old losses against current income.

As of this writing, Lionel has had four consecutively higher offers for its Dale stock. In March 1983, a $43 million offer for Lionel's Dale holdings was received from Acme-Cleveland. On February 24, 1984, Lionel agreed to sell Dale to Dynamics Corporation of America (DCA) for $59.5 million. In April 1984, Lionel asked the bankruptcy court to declare the earlier agreement with DCA nonbinding so that it could accept a $67 million offer from Square D Company for Dale. Finally, in July 1984, Lionel received an offer of $82 million from Charterhouse Group. In just sixteen months, the perceived value of Lionel's Dale holding had doubled. Cash received from selling Dale Electronics constitutes the core of Lionel's reorganization plan. In fact, most successful reorganizations involve valuable assets that may either be sold to raise capital, as in the case of Lionel, or that may be retained in the reorganized firm and later sold, as in the case of Penn Central Railroad. Given a choice, any bankrupt company, including Lionel, would prefer not to sell valuable assets; however, Lionel's stake in Dale Electronics had to be sold to generate cash to satisfy creditors and keep Lionel operating.

In March 1984, Lionel filed a Second Amended Consolidated Plan of Reorganization in bankruptcy court. If the sale of Dale to Charterhouse Group is approved, a third plan will be produced at a later date. The reorganization plan is summarized in table 3–4. The first two columns list Lionel's original capital (debt and equity). The next three columns list what cash, stock, or warrants each class of creditors would receive in the reorganization. At the time the plan was proposed, Lionel's common stock was trading at about $4 per share. Using this per share value to evaluate the plan, the class of general unsecured creditors would receive nearly all the money owed. About three-fourths of the settlement would be cash. However, these creditors will have lost the use of

Table 3–4
Lionel's Second Amended Reorganization Plan
(millions)

	Original Capital		Reorganization Plan Allocation		
Creditors	Debt	Stock	Cash	Stock	Warrants[a]
General unsecured	$100		$74.6	5.3	
Subordinated debenture	$15		All unpaid interest		
Stockholders		7.1		7.1	1.8

[a]A warrant is a long-term stock option allowing the purchase of a share of stock at a pre-specified price. These warrants permit 900,000 shres to be purchased at $8 for up to one year and 900,000 shares to be purchased at $12 over the next eighteen months.

their funds for the time involved in Lionel's reorganization. Holders of the subordinated debentures would receive back interest, and their debt would be reinstated. Finally, the common stockholders would own at least 56 percent of the reorganized company (assuming that warrants are not exercised) and 62.6 percent if they chose to exercise their warrants.

This reorganization plan had been approved by both the creditors' and shareholders' committees that negotiate the plans form and substance. I think it represents a good example of an eminently fair plan. First, creditors receive back most, if not all, of their money. Second, after the reorganization, current stockholders own a majority of the firm. Why, you might ask, should shareholders lose any of their company? The answers to this frequently asked question are straightforward:

1. Their company had failed to meet all its obligations.
2. Only by giving 5.3 million shares of stock to creditors can the company's debts be paid. In other cases where the failed company has less valuable assets, original shareholders may lose all or nearly all of their shares. A good example of this is the Braniff bankruptcy (discussed in chapter 5).

It is interesting to speculate about the shape of a Third Amended Consolidated Plan of Reorganization that would be prepared if the $82 million offer for Dale Electronics is accepted. Compared to the Dale transaction anticipated by the second amended plan, Lionel receives nearly $15 million more in cash. Valuing the common stock at about $4 per share suggests that if the general creditors were given these additional funds, only 1.5 million shares would need to be given to creditors. As a result, current stockholders would retain ownership equivalent to 82.5

percent. Therefore, the newest proposal is better for existing share-holders and for the class of general creditors who would receive more cash. In summary, the more valuable assets are, the less harmful will be the eventual resolution of a bankruptcy.

Synopsis

Cash-flow cycles are a business reality. They lead to trouble only when sales are highly seasonal or when annual cash flow is negative. With proper management, the cash-flow cycle is easily overcome even when sales follow a seasonal pattern; however, as the Charter and Lionel examples illustrate, trouble awaits firms that mismanage the cash-flow cycle.

The first step in cash-flow management is to understand the nature and severity of the problem. The firm must begin by organizing the information needed to react to the problem. This means that the manager must chart out, on a monthly or weekly basis, anticipated cash receipts and cash disbursements. The difference between receipts and disbursements equals cash flow. When cash flow is positive, funds are flowing into the company; when cash flow is negative, funds flow out.

Cash flow and profit are not the same. Profit equals the difference between sales and cost. While at first glance it appears that the two concepts, cash flow and profit, are the same, there is one major difference between the two: cash flow considers only money actually entering or leaving the company, while profit is calculated without considering whether funds have actually been received or disbursed. As a result of this difference, it is possible for a profitable company to have negative cash flow. In other words, the company would be profitable, but at the end of each week or month, there would be less money in the company's bank account to pay for expenses and growth.

The second step in cash-flow management is to develop a plan for meeting the company's cash needs. Usually this involves consulting with lenders and arranging a suitable credit line to meet cash requirements. In addition to looking at the company's projected cash flows, lenders will want to examine the long-term plan for new product development, market expansion, cost control, and other relevant factors.

Essentially there are three possible cash-flow problems: continuously positive cash flows, fluctuating positive and negative cash flows, and continuously negative cash flows. The task of dealing with positive cash flows is one most businesses relish. Not only is a lender superfluous, but the company in effect becomes a lender, looking for good projects in which to invest excess capital.

Fluctuating positive and negative cash flows are fairly typical of seasonal businesses. During the slow season, cash flows are negative. In the high season, cash flows are positive. Lenders are usually willing to advance a profitable, seasonal business sufficient funds to allow it to meet its cash needs during the slow season so that it can earn its expected profits during the high season.

It is harder to obtain funds to meet a continuously negative cash flow. Lenders must be convinced that the firm is currently profitable or else will soon be before they will commit any funds. A profitable company engaged in substantial capital investment projects or in extending credit to its customers may well have negative cash flows. Before lending to this profitable company, creditors will probably want to be convinced that the capital investment project is worthwhile or that the firm needs to be extending as much credit.

I would estimate that more businesses fail because they have lost sight of their cash-flow problem or because they have lost the faith of their lenders than for any other single cause. Many of these failures are unnecessary. To stay on top of the cash-flow problem, many business people have acquired personal computers and spread-sheet programs. With a good spread-sheet program, it is relatively simple to consider every conceivable cash-flow outcome. Armed with this information, every worthy business should be able to acquire funds to meet its cash-flow needs.

4
Getting Buried under Current Assets

A business must have assets. Like vitamins on cereal, assets fortify business. Assets are the items of value a company owns. Assets are acquired because they have earning power, and with them, profits can be made. In fact, by following two simple asset use rules, a business can earn greater profits:

1. Assets should never be idle or be misused.
2. The firm must find and select the best mix of current and long-term assets.

The management of assets is a full-time job; mismanaging assets wastes potential profits and may result in bankruptcy.

Allowing assets to be idle is the surest route to financial disaster (except for farmers who receive government payments for not growing food). The reason is obvious: firms must raise capital in order to be able to afford new assets. Typically money is raised by selling stock or by assuming more debt. Whether money is obtained through the sale of stock or from debt, it is not free; money has a cost to the firm. Unless the assets purchased with the money earn a profit, the business will eventually be in financial trouble. The concept is easier to understand in terms of an individual household. An example of a person wasting assets would be someone buying lottery tickets with his or her paycheck without ever winning. For a while, the person might withdraw cash savings to pay bills, but eventually, when savings are depleted, a financial crisis ensues.

Although businesses do not usually purchase lottery tickets, some corporate decisions yield business strategies that are about as valuable as losing lottery tickets. For example, Mobil, flush with oil profits, acquired Montgomery Ward in a bid to diversify its assets. Apparently Ward has never earned any profit for Mobil and instead has required cash infusions. The Montgomery Ward acquisition in all probability was a mistake.

The mix of corporate assets is a less obvious but perhaps more frequent contributor to business failure than are wasted assets. *Mix of assets* refers to how many dollars are invested in current assets (those convertible into cash within a year) versus dollars invested in long-term or fixed assets. Not only must a firm choose the number of dollars to invest in total assets, but it must also decide whether to invest in inventories or accounts receivable, the principal current assets, or in plant and equipment, the long-term assets. The implications of this choice are significant.

Firms do not choose between doing without current assets or having only current assets. Instead they choose the pecentage, 10 percent or 20 percent or even 30 percent, of total assets to be invested in inventory and accounts receivable. Once a desired current asset ratio is selected, current assets are allowed to grow as the firm's sales and total assets grow.

Current and fixed assets have different profitability and bankruptcy potential characteristics, as shown in table 4–1. Current assets yield relatively low returns, meaning a low profit rate, but they are relatively low-risk investments because of their ready convertibility into cash. In contrast, fixed assets embody both high risk and high profitability.

Inventories and accounts receivable have low profit potentials because they function mostly to facilitate product sales. Fixed assets—the firm's factory, patents, and equipment—have high profit potential because they produce the items to be sold. Customers pay for products, not for inventory or the credit extended. It is the manufacture of products that leads to profits. If this were not true, it would make sense for firms to buy products elsewhere and then merely market them. Although some firms do not have a production base, most companies make what they sell.

Fixed assets have a higher bankruptcy risk than current assets because they are less liquid; it is harder to sell manufacturing plants or used equipment than it is to sell excess inventory or to factor (sell at a discount) receivables. Consider the hypothetical case of mining equipment that had been lowered into a silver mine in Colorado many years ago. While the mine operated, it was extremely profitable; the owners earned a high return on their fixed investment. When silver prices fell, the mine was closed. The equipment would have been useful in other mines

Table 4–1
Profitability and Risk Potential of Current and Fixed Assets

	Current Assets	*Fixed Assets*
Profitability profile	Low returns	High returns
Risk potential	Low risk	High risk

producing different ores, but transportation costs were too high, and the machines were left to rust at the bottom of the pit. Thus, considering the asset over its lifetime, we see that the increased risk of fixed assets is compensated for by the higher profits they are capable of earning.

The bankruptcy risk created by the mix of assets is a two-edged sword. Bankruptcy may eventuate from the asset mix's being too heavily weighted toward current assets or too heavily weighted toward fixed assets. As depicted in figure 4–1, there is a substantial region of acceptable or trouble-free asset mixes, and it is only when the firm goes too far in one direction or the other that problems arise. Poor planning or unmet expectations are usually responsible for asset mix difficulties.

Bowmar Instruments   Eagle ⟶ Dinosaur
Too Many Current Assets

Bowmar Instruments, a technology-based firm most frequently remembered for its Bowmar Brain calculators, went bankrupt in February 1975. Although Bowmar did not develop the first hand-held calculator, it pioneered the commercialization and product marketing of this new idea. The future must have seemed promising to Bowmar executives. Sales rose to $65 million in 1973 from $13 million in 1971. Bowmar's common stock was even more glamorous, rising as much as $5 in a single day as investors viewed the company as the "next Xerox." Not wanting to be left behind, investors drove up the stock price to $45 per

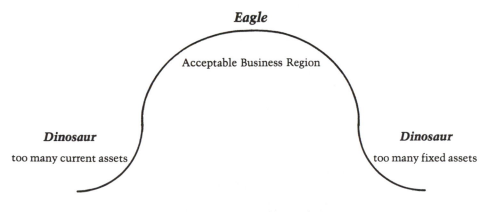

Figure 4–1. Asset Mix

share. At this point, the stock market valued Bowmar as worth approximately $90 million ($45 per share for 2 million shares).

Planning Bowmar's future must have been exhilarating. Like any other pioneer, however, the company was venturing into new territory and thus encountered unexpected dangers. In retrospect, we know that new competitors, Texas Instruments and Hewlett Packard among others, aggressively entered the calculator market, introducing new products with expanded capabilities, and drove down the prices charged by the industry. Falling prices may help profits if enough new sales offset lower revenue from old customers; however, for several reasons, falling prices are more likely to harm profits than boost them.

When prices fall, each unit sale makes a lower contribution to profits. The profit contribution equals the difference between price and cost. If prices fall to the same level as cost, the firm breaks even on each unit. Profits could not be produced at any output level.

The second harm caused by falling prices is to diminish the value of raw material, work-in-progress, and finished goods inventory. If the market price of products declines, the value of the firm's inventory declines by an equal percentage amount. Each dollar loss in inventory value also causes a dollar loss in the firm's equity or net worth. Since assets equal the sum of liabilities and net worth, with a large enough fall in prices, the decrease in inventory value can bankrupt a company.

In Bowmar's case, when the competition's new products hit the market, Bowmar was unable to respond adequately. Bowmar was limited by a stockpile of older, relatively high-priced integrated circuits. It had invested too heavily in current assets; specifically it held too much inventory with the wrong chracteristics. When the price of integrated circuits fell, the market value of Bowmar's circuits in inventory plummeted. Table 4–2 compares Bowmar's annual sales and inventory levels. What must have happened is that Bowmar's executives expected the dollar value of sales to continue growing at historic rates and did not anticipate falling prices or inventory values. Thus, when the dollar value of sales precipitously declined beginning late in 1973 (unit sales were stronger), Bowmar was left with too much inventory. In the three-year period ending in 1973, Bowmar averaged $3.88 of sales for every dollar of inventory. In 1974, only $1.13 of sales occurred for each dollar of inventory. Since profits are earned selling goods and not by holding inventory, Bowmar had gotten buried under its current assets.

By analogy, companies marketing wine products know not to overstock inventories of faddish products such as youth wines or near beers. Sales and profits can be realized on these products for a time, but ultimately their appeal fades, and their value diminishes. Bowmar

Table 4–2
Bowmar Instruments' Annual Sales and Inventory
(millions of dollars)

	Sales	Inventory	Sales/Inventory
1971	$13	$ 3	4.33
1972	31	8	3.88
1973	65	19	3.42
1974	26	23	1.13

might have endured had it known how rapidly the value of integrated circuits could fall and had it maintained a leaner current asset balance.

Current asset management is not simple. The proper strategy is not just to maintain a limited or minimal level of inventories or accounts receivable. The other side of the two-edged asset mix sword may inflict harm if too few current assets are held relative to a firm's total assets. The firm must position itself in the middle-range area of figure 4–1 even though it is unaware of future product, economic, environmental, or sociological developments. Like a soldier, it must be adequately equipped to fight but resourceful and lean enough to respond to changes in the battlefield if it is to survive.

Consider a possible sequence of events had Bowmar maintained lean current assets, particularly inventories. It may not have been able to produce enough calculators to meet consumer demand. In some markets, having unsatisfied demand increases consumers' perceptions of the products value. For example, Saab of America runs out of Saab motorcars to sell by May or June in most years. Consumers who might have purchased a Saab in the summer may instead buy an available Chevrolet or Ford, but usually they react by increasing their assessment of the product's value and wait until the next model year to buy a Saab. Calculators, however, are not the sort of product that consumers will wait for. A calculator is a tool; without one, productivity suffers. Moreover, Bowmar's calculators were not the only ones available. Other calculators were on the market, and even if other manufacturers had adopted similar strategies and had also run out of products, new competitors would have promptly sprung up since the technology to assemble the product was not proprietary. In fact, heightened competition might have caused calculator prices to plummet sooner than they actually did. Lower product prices may also have led to Bowmar's failure. Clearly the asset mix sword is two edged, with too few and too many current assets both being dangerous.

Like other bankruptcies, there are many good explanations for Bowmar's failure. It might be said that Bowmar lacked sufficient owners' capital (equity). With more equity, the inventory difficulties could have been overcome, and new products could have been introduced to the market bearing Bowmar's established product name. (The capital investment issue is pursued in chapter 6.)

Alternatively Bowmar's collapse may be attributed exclusively to the rapid decline in price that affected its product. Machines that once sold for $100 to $150 sold several years later for just $10. Or it might be said that poor management caused Bowmar to fail. After all, other calculator companies survived and prospered in an environment of $10 calculators. Price skimming (charging a very high price for new products) is a well-established technique, and the firm's managers should have known that as competitors enter a market, prices generally fall. For example, ballpoint pens that now sell for well under $1 sold for more than $50 when they were first introduced in the 1950s. Once people willing to pay an exorbitant price to be the first person with a new product have been satisfied, price tends to fall to a level closer to cost. Whether profits fall or rise depends on consumers' reactions to the lower price. If sales rise enough, profits may actually be higher at a lower price.

W.T. Grant   Tortoise ⟶ Dinosaur
Too Many and Then Too Few Current Assets

W.T. Grant went bankrupt in 1975. At that time, the Grant bankruptcy had the distinction of being the largest corporate bankruptcy on record. With 82,000 employees, 1,200 stores, and over $1.6 billion in sales, Grant was a major presence in retailing. More than half of the stores had been opened during the prior decade. Sales rose dramatically as the firm expanded. As we shall see—and this makes the Grant case quite interesting—the company initially got into financial trouble by having *too many* current assets, but the ultimate liquidation of the firm occurred because it had *too few* current assets.

Grant was competing in a tough market. Sears, K-Mart, Montgomery Ward, and JCPenney comprise a solid core of retailers with loyal consumers. To attract consumers away from more established firms (Grant was in fact organized around the turn of the century), Grant developed a reputation for providing easy credit. Credit was not administered centrally but was granted by each store. Credit customers were given up to thirty-six months to pay and had minimum monthly payments of as little as $1. While the availability of lenient credit terms and more retail

Table 4–3
W.T. Grant's Sales and Income, Year Ending January 31
(millions of dollars)

	1968	1969	1970	1971	1972	1973	1974	1975
Sales	$979.5	$1,096.2	$1,210.9	$1,254.1	$1,374.8	$1,644.7	$1,849.8	$1,762.0
Income	33.0	38.2	41.8	36.4	31.6	35.0	10.9	(177.3)

locations caused sales to grow, as seen in table 4–3, some of the credit sales were uncollectible (table 4–4). Credit had been given to high-risk customers, some of whom were deadbeats. In 1975, for example, almost 20 percent of account receivables were considered uncollectible. Current assets, notably account receivables, were too high.

When banks and other lenders eventually recognized Grant's dilemma, it was too late. Part of the blame for this delayed response was due to the fact that Grant leased nearly 90 percent of its stores. At that time, lease obligations, as opposed to borrowed money or money raised by selling stock, were not reported on balance sheets as corporate liabilities. Today lease obligations are now more accurately reported as long-term debt.

Lenders first reduced the supply of credit to Grant and then took steps leading to new management. The new managers closed unprofitable stores and limited the product lines offered at remaining outlets. The stores suffered physically as a result of the austerity program. Given a choice between shopping in dingy and sparsely outfitted Grant stores or at a competitor's, consumers went elsewhere. As a result, sales at Grant trailed off. Suppliers noticed the change. They had granted over $150 million in credit to Grant in 1975 but grew wary and started to withhold deliveries. Shelves became even more depleted. The situation became hopeless, and eventually Grant filed for bankruptcy court protection. By the time a reorganization plan could be considered, Grant's good name was gone. The final death bell was rung because there were too few current assets—not enough goods on the shelves.

The sale of all of Grant's assets raised approximately $320 million. As of 1975, the firm had liabilities of approximately $968 million. Thus, about thirty-three cents on the dollar was available to pay off liabilities. Creditors do not stand as equals in line for repayment, however. Some are higher on a priority list than others (refer to table 1–4 for an outline of the recognized priority of creditors' claims). Given the amount of money available, the creditors' committee, not too surprisingly, voted to liquidate Grant's assets. Stockholders were left without anything.

Table 4–4
W.T. Grant's Credit Data, Year Ending January 31
(millions of dollars)

	1970	1971	1972	1973	1974	1975
Accounts receivable	$368.3	$358.4	$408.3	$468.6	$540.8	$431.2
Uncollectible accounts	15.3	15.5	15.8	15.8	16.3	79.5

Synopsis

The two most important current assets are inventories and accounts receivable. Inventories are a supply of goods to sell or in the process of being produced; accounts receivable is the credit offered to consumers. Firms could not operate without either. If either accounts receivable or inventories leave the acceptable business region (see figure 4–1), a firm is likely to fail.

As the Bowmar and Grant cases illustrate, managers may unknowingly permit current assets to become too large relative to total assets. Among the forces that may encourage too great an investment in current assets are the following frequently encountered business situations.

A long period of sustained growth.

Economies of scale in production, which encourage size before sales.

Liberalization of accounts receivable credit terms.

An economic slowdown, which reduces the rate at which receivables are paid off.

With excessive current asset investment, the business may lose sight of its actual size and instead focus on how large it anticipates becoming. When this occurs, if the firm fails to achieve its growth target, current assets will be too large.

In order to avoid getting buried under current assets, the best strategy is to monitor both inventories and accounts receivable by comparing their size to the firm's investment in total assets. Once the ratio of inventory or accounts receivable to total assets rises, thoughtful decisions needed to be reached concerning whether this increase is willful and desired or is unplanned and harmful.

5
Getting Squeezed by Equipment

E very day we all make trade-offs. When we buy a new car, we understand that the model with the highest miles-per-gallon rating will not be the most comfortable or easy to handle. In purchasing a new home with a limited budget, we may trade an extra bedroom for what we perceive as a better neighborhood. Businesses also confront choices. One of the most important business choices concerns the number (or cost) and sophistication of machines used in producing the firm's product. As a result of poor choices, firms have gone bankrupt: they have been squeezed by their own equipment.

Machines appear on a company's balance sheet as fixed assets. The term *fixed assets* arose because the costs associated with machines—depreciation, maintenance, taxes, and so forth—are fixed and will be incurred whether the firm uses or needs the assets. In contrast, labor costs can be lowered during slack periods by laying off workers, fuel costs can be reduced by turning off the heat, and raw materials costs can be controlled by producing out of inventories. Labor, fuel, and materials are all *variable-cost items*; the total number of dollars spent on each rises and falls directly with the level of the firm's output. When the firm increases output, more workers are hired, leading to an increased wage bill. And, fuel and material costs increase when output increases and decrease when output decreases.

U.S. business firms spent over $50 billion on new equipment in 1983. This investment surge is partly responsible for the successful U.S. economic recovery experienced in 1983 and 1984. Capital investment on machines raises fixed costs, but it also lowers the cost of producing more output. Thus, when a company purchases new machines, it has higher fixed costs that need to be paid but lower incremental costs (the cost of making additional units of output). Financial analysts use the phrase *operating leverage* to describe the production consequences of trading off fixed costs (machines) for variable costs, such as labor or energy. When more machines are used, the company's operating leverage is said to increase. Some industries tend to be more capital (machine) intensive than others. For example, steel mills and oil refineries must expend millions of dollars on machinery to operate; those industries are characterized as using high operating leverage. Similarly, some countries, notably Japan, use more capital. As a result, Japanese industries have lower variable production cost than U.S. firms.

Operating leverage describes what happens to operating *profit* (revenues less all costs except financing costs) as sales increase. As sales increase, a firm with high operating leverage has a greater increase in operating profits than a firm with lower operating leverage. If sales fall, this firm's operating profits quickly decrease and can become losses. Machinery cannot be laid off in slow times. Thus, the airline industry, which tends toward high operating leverage, experiences both profitable years and losing years as the economy moves through its cycles. Eastern Airlines, for example, was profitable when the economy was strong in 1977, 1978, and 1979, earning, respectively, $1.38, $2.91, and $2.10 per share. During the next three years, the economy collapsed, and Eastern lost money in each of these years: $1.76, $2.69, and $3.22 per share in 1980, 1981, and 1982, respectively.

Figure 5–1 illustrates the consequences of the fixed-variable cost trade-off. Firm A, described at the top of the figure, has invested $1 million in machines; firm B, in the same industry as firm A, invested only $75,000 on fixed-cost items. The cost difference between the high and low capital cost choices may be closer than those depicted in figure 5–1 and still have a significant impact. (It should be pointed out that although a decision to spend $1 million or only $75,000 on machines depends as well on the company's ability to finance the purchase, this chapter examines only the leverage aspect of the problem. The leverage problem is related to the asset level problem, but it is not the same issue.)

What does firm A receive as a result of spending the extra $925,000 on fixed assets? The answer to this important question is found by comparing the cost curves in the figure. Notice how the cost curve in the top half of the figure is very flat; the cost of making no output—$1 million—is close to the cost of making 700,000 units—1.05 million. As a result of making 700,000 pieces of goods, costs increase by only 5 percent—not a bad trade-off.

In the lower half of the figure, in contrast, merely increasing production from the zero, or no output, level, up to 10,000 units causes cost to double from $75,000 to $150,000. This comparison demonstrates that expensive machines usually allow firms to expand output at lower additional cost. The reverse also holds true: by economizing on the amount of money invested in machines, a firm must spend more to increase its output.

The cost per unit of expanding output depends on the firm's investment in capital. For firm A, which made the $1 million capital investment, costs increase by $50,000 when output increases by 700,000 units. As table 5–1 shows, this firm spends about $0.72 for each extra unit

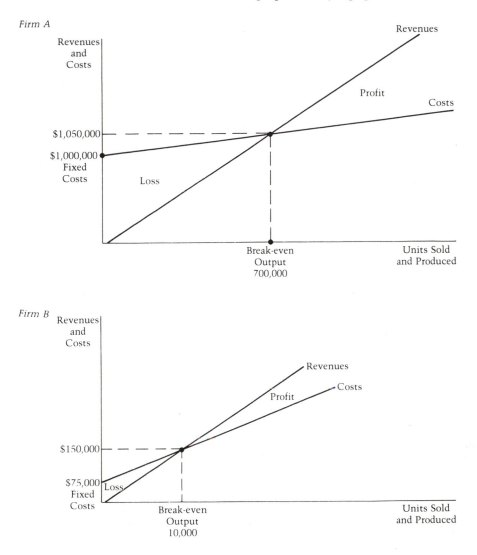

Figure 5–1. Comparison of High- and Low-Fixed-Cost Companies

produced. Alternatively, firm B, spending only $75,000 on machines, pays $7.50 for each extra unit produced. For the companies described in figure 5–1, management's choices are to buy an expensive machine capable of turning out products at $0.72 apiece, or to buy a less expensive machine that produces output at $7.50 per unit. Which is the correct choice? Stated in these terms, the matter seems quite clear, but in fact, more information is needed.

Table 5–1
Calculating the Cost of Increasing Output

	Expensive Machine	Inexpensive Machine
Increase in cost	$50,000	$75,000
Increase in output	700,000 units	10,000 units
Cost per unit	$0.72	$7.50

In addition to considering differences in investment costs and incremental production costs, the business person also needs to calculate the *break-even output* for each type of machine. Break-even output equals the number of units the firm must produce and sell in order to pay for the machine's fixed and variable costs. Only after selling these units does the firm start to make an operating profit that can be used to pay interest to debt holders or to distribute dividends to owners. Break-even output is found by comparing fixed costs to the number of dollars earned from selling the product after paying variable cost. To keep the analysis as simple as possible, we will assume that fixed cost equals investment costs. If the machine lasts but one year, this simplifying assumption is closer to the truth. Table 5–2 illustrates break-even output calculations for the two machines being considered, one costing $1 million and the other costing $75,000.

Contribution margin is found in table 5–2 by subtracting the variable cost per unit of running the machine from the product's selling price. Since both machines have been assumed to produce the same product, the output from each sells for the same price, $15.00 per unit. When the $1 million machine is purchased, the firm has a high contribution

Table 5–2
Calculating Break-even Output by Using Contribution Margin and Cost

	Expensive Machine	Inexpensive Machine
Inputs		
Price per unit sold	$15.00	$15.00
Variable cost per unit of running machine	$0.72	$7.50
Contribution margin	$14.28	$7.50
Cost of machine	$1,000,000	$75,000
Output		
Break-even output	700,000 units	10,000 units

Note: Break-even output = Cost of machine or annual fixed cost/contribution margin.

margin—$14.28 per unit produced—because of the low variable cost. A far smaller contribution margin—$7.50 per unit—results when the less expensive machine is purchased. If the product has the same price on store shelves regardless of which machine is used to produce it, why are the contribution margins different? What differs between the two cases is how much the firm spends additionally (incrementally) to turn out the product after buying the machine of its choice.

Obviously if the two machines had the same break-even output, the one with the higher contribution margin would be purchased; however, break-even output is usually higher for machines with higher contribution margins. The choice between the two machines depends on break-even output and on the output the company reasonably expects to sell. A high contribution margin has little value if expected output is too low ever to allow the firm to reach break-even. Table 5–3 summarizes the decision using the final factor, the level of operating profit.

Operating profit equals total revenue minus all costs, except for the cost of financing the firm. All other things being equal, a higher operating profit is better. All other things are rarely the same, however. To obtain higher operating profits, the firm must buy more machines, and thus its finance charges increase while net earnings may fall.

Operating profit varies with output. In fact, the rate at which operating profit changes as output changes is exactly equal to the firm's contribution margin. A higher contribution margin leads to a more rapid change in operating profits as sales change. Profits fall when output falls and rise when output rises.

The firm decides between the two machines—one costing $1 million and the other costing just $75,000—by considering the profit-making potential of each as shown in table 5–3. With the expensive machine,

Table 5–3
Operating Profit/Loss

Expected Output	Expensive Machine	Inexpensive Machine
10,000 units	$ −851,714	$ 0
400,000 units	−428,571	213,000
700,000 units	0	429,000
1,400,000 units	18,992,000	933,000
5,000,000 units	70,400,000	3,525,000

Note: Example calculation for an expensive machine where output is 1,400,000 units, price is $15, fixed cost is $1,000,000, and variable cost is $0.72:

$$\text{operating profit} = \text{revenue} - \text{fixed cost} - \text{variable cost}$$
$$= \$21,000,000 - \$1,000,000 - \$1,008,000$$
$$= \$18,992,000$$

the firm has an operating loss at relatively low output levels—fewer than 700,000 units. Once it is past the break-even point, however, operating profits explode, reaching $70 million at an output of 5 million units. By contrast, the less expensive machine's break-even point is only 10,000 units. Thus, it is easier to not lose money with the less costly equipment. But in exchange, it is harder to do well with this equipment. Even at an output of 5 million units, only $3.5 million in operating profit is earned. This is just 5 percent of what might be earned with the better machine.

Which of the two machines should be purchased? The correct choice hinges on the number of finished units that will be sold. Lacking a working crystal ball, business managers estimate sales using their experience, marketing research data, trade group information, and whatever other reliable data are available. Sales forecasting is a thankless job. When the forecast is on target, everyone assumes the task was easy. When it is off target, the forecaster stands alone; people tend not to share failure.

If both machines produce a specialty product with potential annual sales of about 400,000 units, the $75,000 machine should be acquired since it reaches break-even output quicker. If all the estimates—sales, price per unit, cost of producing output—hold, the firm should make about $213,000 in operating income. If these are mass production machines, however, and annual sales of about 5 million units are anticipated, the $1 million machine is better. Assuming the estimate is accurate, an operating profit of almost $71 million would be earned.

Whether the business person is considering the acquisition of an expensive machine or an inexpensive machine or is looking at the purchase of one machine versus ten machines (all costing the same amount), inaccurate or misleading information may lead to the wrong number of machines being acquired. Although firms should not strive to underpurchase machines, the consequences of inadequate capital investment are not as harmful as having too much invested in machines.

When a firm starts with too few machines, production quickly reaches the limits of capacity, and there are benefits to producing at full capacity. But if the market is not completely satisfied, an opportunity is created for potential competitors to enter the market. Future profits might be lower if there are more producers in the market. More important, if the firm is producing at capacity, it is probably forgoing sales that could have been made had there been extra productive capacity. Since profits increase with output, reaching full capacity means that the firm's profit potential has not been reached. Thus, underpredicting sales and underbuilding capacity is not costless, though the cost may be invisible.

On the other hand, overpredicting sales results in the acquisition of too much capital equipment and creates the potential for a firm to be squeezed by its own equipment. Operating profits will be lower than expected and may even be negative. Sometimes excess capacity can be sold off. This is likely if excess capacity coincides with someone else's undercapacity or if the plant or equipment can be modified to turn out another product. If excess capacity is sold, costs are reduced and the firm may survive.

When a firm is unable to unload superfluous facilities or machines, it must still continue to pay off creditors whose loaned funds enabled the company to make the capital purchase. How the firm responds to this crisis and how soon it takes action in all likelihood will determine whether it will survive. The first step to take is to lower variable cost by laying off workers and by curtailing other expenses. Next, the machines or plant must be put up for sale, or if a sales rebound is expected, they should be mothballed. The firm's *financial reserves* (unused credit capacity) must be used to meet debt obligations. If reserves expire before business improves, bankruptcy may result.

Braniff Airways Eagle ⟶ Dinosaur

Braniff Airways was a success in the 1960s. Spurred by a population shift into the sunbelt region of the United States and by novel marketing techniques, including airplanes painted by the artist Calder and leather seats, Braniff took off from modest beginnings to become one of the nine trunkline air carriers in the United States.

The air travel business environment had been overseen by the Civil Aeronautics Board (CAB), the federal airline regulator. Not only were airlines assigned routes, but the CAB also established prices. The CAB exchanged subsidies for taxes to reach its objectives. For example, by agreeing to operate an unprofitable route—perhaps Minneapolis to Houston—an airline would receive in exchange a profitable route—such as Chicago to Dallas—to compensate for the other route's losses. Airline managers learned to play the regulation game and to negotiate a better route system in exchange for serving politically powerful and yet unprofitable routes.

Since the number of carriers serving any route was fixed by the CAB and since all carriers charged the same prices, success depended on using competitive practices other than price discounts to attract passengers. Marketing was the name of the game. Little attention was given to cost control, improved efficiency, capacity planning, or optimal routing.

Seeking growth in a regulated environment, Braniff tried the small advertising firm of Wells, Rich and Greene Inc. because of its fresh ideas. Things clicked. For a time, Braniff was the fastest-growing U.S. airline and one of the most prosperous. The close relationship between Braniff and Wells, Rich and Greene finally culminated in the marriage of the chairman of Braniff and the president of the ad agency.

Late in the 1970s, it became clear that the CAB was being put out of business by the deregulation movement sweeping Congress. Many airlines chose to wait out the first round of deregulation to observe its impact, but Braniff moved aggressively. Of 1,300 routes opened up by the CAB, Braniff began flying in almost 400. Overnight its scheduled number of flights doubled. To meet the equipment need, Braniff acquired eight new 747 aircraft at a cost in excess of $900 million. Braniff must have been forecasting a tremendous growth in demand. Thus, the use of high operating leverage seemed appropriate. Unfortunately for Braniff, the forecast was wrong.

Braniff's entry into new air markets did not go unnoticed. Airlines already serving those routes responded to maintain their market share. Most added extra flights and cut their prices, and soon fare wars became contagious. The challenger, Braniff, failed to win over enough consumers to reach break-even. The firm was not profitable; in fact, it was operating at a loss.

If Braniff had entered these markets without expanding its fleet of aircraft, it might have been able to retreat back to its own profitable routes. Instead Braniff had to continue to pay interest and lease charges on newly acquired planes. Moreover, the market for used aircraft almost evaporated as competitors noticed Braniff's inability to increase profits by expanding in the new deregulation era. After holding on for some time, Braniff finally filed a Chapter 11 bankruptcy petition on May 13, 1982. The firm had succumbed to having too many machines. The Braniff that flies today (late 1984) has a different ownership structure from the old Braniff. A company controlled by Hyatt Inc. gave Braniff a cash infusion, and old debtors took stock in the new company. Original shareholders today own but a small piece of the new Braniff. Their ownership was lowered by a reverse stock split in which old stock was returned in exchange for fewer shares of new stock.

International Harvester   Eagle ⟶ Dinosaur

International Harvester (IHC) is another example of a firm that got squeezed by its own equipment. Although IHC has never sought court protection from creditors as Braniff did, it is nonetheless an economic failure, having lost an extraordinary amount of money in the past four years and having been close to (if not actually at) technical insolvency in 1983. Like Chrysler and Continental Illinois Bank, an IHC failure might damage other sectors of the economy by causing related firms to fail and thereby costing workers and small business people their livelihood. Despite the risk, the government has not rescued IHC as it did both Chrysler and Continental Bank. Instead, an out-of-court solution has apparently been found. Before this, a turnaround was promised by IHC if only its creditors would be patient. When progress toward profitability was slow to materialize, it was still not necessary to declare bankruptcy because creditors realized they would recoup more of their investment if IHC were kept alive than if they forced the firm to seek court protection.

IHC's demise represents a good example of how operating leverage may lead to either higher or lower profits. Operating leverage describes the relationship between a firm's fixed costs and its variable costs or its operating income and sales. Technically, operating leverage is calculated as the percentage change in operating profits (revenue less all costs except finance charges and taxes) that results from a 1 percent change in sales. Thus, a firm with an operating leverage of 1.5 will experience a 1.5 percent increase in operating profit for every 1 percent increase in sales (for example, a 10 percent sales rise increases profits by 15 percent). Had IHC's sales not fallen, today's red ink might have been black, and the IHC story would not have belonged in this book.

The year 1974 was pivotal for the company. In that year, IHC had $4.9 billion in gross revenue, with operations extending into both the truck and agricultural equipment businesses. The IHC label was carried on products ranging from gasoline and diesel-powered trucks and tractors to school bus chassis and agricultural implements, and these products all had wide market acceptance. Operating profits exceeded $300 million, and net income was nearly $118 million.

Although IHC's financial performance was reasonably good, the national economic and social environment in which it operated was in an upheaval resulting from the Arab oil embargo begun in October 1973. How this event would produce permanent changes in practically every facet of existence was only beginning to emerge. Yet there seemed to be cause for optimism at IHC; after all, profits were up despite a major economic recession in 1974. (Earnings per share were $4.24 in 1974 compared to $3.86 in 1973.) At this juncture IHC began implementation of a critical decision made within the higher echelons of its management: to accelerate capital spending on plant and equipment. The specific reasons for promulgating this plan are company confidential, but we can speculate about the motives. Higher gasoline and diesel fuel prices resulted from the escalation in crude oil prices that followed the oil embargo. Truck operators and other users of IHC products were clamoring for vehicles with improved fuel efficiency and seemed willing to invest in new, upgraded fleets of vehicles. In order to be able to meet an expected surge in demand, IHC commenced an expensive modernization and expansion program.

IHC spent $175 million for capital equipment in both 1974 and 1975. The relative size of the expansion program is observed by noting that IHC's 1974 and 1975 capital spending budgets were nearly three times larger than either the 1971 or 1972 budgets. Figure 5–2 helps illustrate the growth in IHC's capital budget by showing this spending as dollars invested per share of common stock.

During the period 1969–1973, the average amount of capital spending per share of common stock was $3.03 annually. This average more than doubled during the next five years, 1974–1978, to $6.26 per share, and then rose by two-thirds again during the next three years, 1979–1981, to $10.46 annually per share. Note as well that over this period the number of common shares increased from 27 million to 32 million.

IHC's cash flow (profits, plus depreciation and other noncash expenses) remained strong. Nonetheless, the company had to assume more long-term debt to help finance the expansion. Table 5–4 ties together many relevant financial statistics.

At first, IHC prospered. Sales rose each year through 1979, with 1979 growth registering a healthy 25 percent gain over 1978. Gross revenues reached nearly $8.4 billion in 1979, almost $3.5 billion above the level

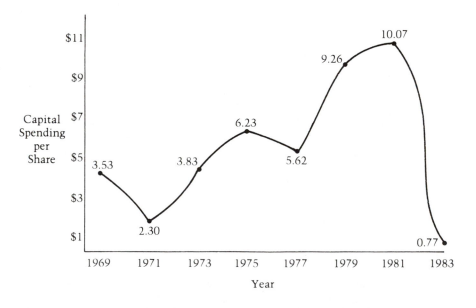

Figure 5–2. International Harvester's Capital Spending per Share of Common Stock

five years earlier. Both operating and net profits increased with sales. Profits do not necessarily rise dollar for dollar with sales. If the company's operating leverage is greater (less) than 1.0, operating profit increases faster (slower) than sales. IHC's profit margins are listed in table 5–5.

Both IHC's operating and net profit margins rose between 1974 and 1979 since IHC had operating leverage above 1.0. Benefits were accruing from the modernization and expansion program. The low cost per unit of producing extra output (alternatively, IHC's high contribution margin) allowed profit margins to increase. The investment community approved of IHC's plan and its consequences. IHC's stock rose from $20 per share at the beginning of 1975 to $40 per share by the end of 1979. IHC's image was of a company with a well-thought-out strategy that might continue to reap benefits from high operating leverage. Over the period 1975–1979, operating income rose 103 percent, while sales increased at a slower 60 percent pace. Operating leverage is calculated by dividing profit growth by sales growth, yielding a 1.71 value for IHC's operating leverage. An operating leverage of 1.71 means that over the period 1975–1979, for each 1 percent growth in sales IHC achieved, operating profits increased by 1.71 percent.

A high degree of operating leverage is beneficial only as long as sales rise. As table 5–4 shows, IHC's plan began to fail when sales declined in 1979. With a high degree of operating leverage, profits quickly become losses when sales decline. In 1980, IHC lost money; operating income was a negative $397.3 million. Sales picked up slightly the next year, producing a modest $14 million in operating income, but high finance charges resulted in a net income deficit of $393 million. Sales plunged in 1982, and the profit picture worsened as the company lost $822 million.

Table 5–4
International Harvester's Financial Data, 1975–1983
(millions of dollars)

	Capital Spending	Change in Long-Term Debt	Sales	Operating Income	Net Income	Cash Flow	Net Worth	Working Capital
1975	$173	$313	$5,246	$414	$ 71	$ 149	$1,443	$1,215
1976	168	(15)	5,488	483	174	259	1,581	1,224
1977	163	3	5,975	543	204	293	1,734	1,276
1978	210	7	6,664	653	187	293	1,876	1,210
1979	285	16	8,392	839	370	491	2,199	1,392
1980	384	379	6,311	—[a]	(397)	(273)	1,897	947
1981	325	658	7,040	14	(393)	(271)	1,482	864
1982	108	30	4,292	—[a]	(822)	(673)	33	521
1983	31	(727)	3,601	14	(434)	(303)	243	21

[a]Deficit.

Table 5–5
International Harvester's Profit Margin

Year	Operating Profit Margin	Net Profit Margin
1974	7.6%	2.4%
1975	7.9	1.4
1976	8.8	3.2
1977	9.1	3.4
1978	9.8	2.8
1979	10.0	4.4
1980	NC	NC
1981	0.2	NC
1982	NC	NC
1983	0.4	NC

Note: NC indicates that profits were less than zero, so the ratio is not calculable.

The year 1983 was no better in terms of sales, but operating profits were in the black again as cutbacks and layoffs lowered costs. Net income, however, remained negative at $434 million; the firm lost $10.69 per share of stock. Net income was a negative $62.8 million through the first nine months of 1984, a vast improvement over the $350 million loss for the same period in 1983. Sales were 34 percent higher during this period.

By the end of 1983, IHC was in dreadful financial shape. Cumulative net losses of $2.05 billion had been incurred in the prior four years, practically equaling IHC's 1979 net worth of $2.2 billion. Moreover, working capital (the difference between current assets and current liabilities) was nearly exhausted, having plunged from $1.4 billion in 1979 to $21 million in 1983. Thus, the firm was virtually at the point of being technically insolvent (working capital was almost negative).

Two managerial options were available:

1. Seek court protection by a Chapter 11 bankruptcy filing and then reorganize the firm.
2. Apprise creditors of the financial dilemma and seek a mutual pact to restructure the firm.

A major advantage favoring the informal plan (option 2) is that substantial costs can be saved by circumventing court-supervised procedures. Also, it is conceivable that an informal restructuring might adopt a plan that, though best for the firm, might be viewed as unfair and thus would be unacceptable to certain classes of creditors or stockholders in a Chapter 11 procedure. IHC chose to negotiate informally with its creditors.

In December 1983, IHC announced that it had obtained approval from all 220 of its lenders, covering $1.4 billion in IHC debt and $2.6 billion of debt issued by its credit subsidiary. Essentially the plan was designed to renew lender confidence in IHC by increasing the level of stockholder capital or equity. The plan promoted a financial redesign and ignored operational issues since IHC had already ended the modernization and expansion program and in fact had been closing older, less efficient facilities. Table 5–6 outlines the proposed plan.

Approximately $500 million dollars of debt was converted into equity as a result of the financial restructuring. This change has two effects. First, equity holders receive dividend payments (if they are declared by the board of directors) instead of interest, which is paid to debt holders. IHC stock had paid dividends equaling as much as $2.35 per share in 1979 but since 1982 had paid no dividend at all. Typically lenders will not permit common stock dividends to be paid if the company is in financial distress. Thus, as a result of converting debt into equity, IHC's losses are lower and its profits higher because interest expense is reduced.

Second, IHC's balance sheet shows more stockholders' equity and net worth as a result of the conversion. Lenders prefer more equity since their debts are more likely to be recovered in full if there is a sizable equity cushion.

Why did some debt holders agree to convert debt into equity? One reason is that they obtained warrants that if converted into common stock will make them majority owners of the company. A second reason for agreeing to convert debt into equity is that had they not agreed, the company would have failed. Debt holders should receive more for their

Table 5–6
International Harvester's Debt Restructuring Plan,
December 15, 1983

Converted Liabilities	New Liabilities
$405 million debt	
$500 million Series B preferred stock	600,298 shares Series E preferred stock[a]
22 million common stock warrants	
$100 million debt	100,000 shares Series E preferred stock[b]

[a]This issue is convertible into 60 million shares of common stock. IHC now has approximately 40 million common shares.

[b]This debt is scheduled to convert in July 1984 after IHC sells additional common stock to the public. These shares convert into 10 million shares of common stock.

securities if IHC survives and prospers than if IHC had been pushed into bankruptcy. Why did existing stockholders accept the plan? IHC might have filed a Chapter 11 bankrupt petition without a restructuring. In a Chapter 11 reorganization, the original common stock may have been worthless.

Synopsis

Long-term assets include land, buildings, equipment, patents, and goodwill. Long-term assets are more profitable than current assets, but long-term assets are also riskier. By deciding to invest more in long-term assets, a company has simultaneously made two decisions: to seek increased profits and to absorb more risk.

Both International Harvester and Braniff adopted strategies that required increased investment in long-term assets. Such strategies work so long as sales grow. If sales fail to increase to the level anticipated, operating profits will fall and may even become losses.

The business person confronts a dilemma. The greatest potential increase in profits comes from additions to fixed assets; however, the risk of failure increases as the firm acquires more long-term assets. Good managers must be willing to assume some of this risk but must be careful not to adopt too much. Unfortunately, there are no fail-safe methods for choosing the right amount of fixed assets since the optimal quantity depends on the unknown level of future sales.

6
Getting Lost with Too Little Capital

Every year several new books are published professing to inform readers how to earn a million dollars through real estate investment. Readers are advised to purchase property with the minimum down payment acceptable to lenders. The authors usually treat 90 percent financing (making a 10 percent down payment) as the lower limit of acceptability and extol 100 percent financing as the supreme objective. The simple premise on which this investment advice is based is that property values rise over time, and therefore in the future the property can be resold at a higher price. The difference between the old and new price is *capital appreciation earned*. It is not dependent on the size of the down payment. By simple division, readers are shown that the percentage return on their investment increases as smaller and smaller original down payments are made. Undoubtedly this strategy has and will work for some investors; however, other investors may find themselves in financial trouble if they use too little capital.

The idea of borrowing money to help finance an acquisition is not unique to real estate. Small business entrepreneurs often borrow start-up funds from friends or relatives, banks lend funds to buyers of expensive artwork, racehorses, and automobiles, and companies borrow money to help pay for purchases of plant and equipment. What distinguishes real estate from other investments is that the investment itself is always viewed as having a resale value, and lenders thus treat the real estate as acceptable collateral. Other investments—for example, a small business—may not have value to anyone other than the current owner, and lenders thus require *external collateral* (such as rights to the owners' home equity) before approving a loan. Ultimately lenders prefer not to fund small business. In part for this reason, small business loan programs have been funded by the federal government.

All businesses must decide how much money to borrow and how much money the owners should invest. The choice is frequently termed *the debt (borrowed money) and equity (owner's money) decision*. One way financial analysts compare companies is to calculate their ratios of debt to equity. Companies with high debt-to-equity ratios are using relatively more borrowed money than those with low debt-to-equity ratios. In the United States, the average company has a 0.50 ratio of debt to equity; that is, the average U.S. company borrows 50 percent of its funds and raises the other 50 percent from owners or retained earnings. In Japan, the ratio is typically much higher. On average, Japanese companies borrow 90 to 95 percent of their capital needs. The reasons for using more debt in Japan are many but included among them are the larger size of Japanese firms, government participation in investment decisions, and the smaller size of the Japanese stock exchange.

Many alternatives are available to companies that need to raise debt and/or equity funds. Some of these are listed and explained in tables 6–1 and 6–2. The most important differences between debt and equity are listed below:

> Debt holders receive interest payments that are a tax-deductible expense to the company. Dividends, by contrast, are a distribution to owners and thus are not tax deductible.

> Nonpayment of interest, except in the case of income bonds, violates loan provisions and may lead to bankruptcy. Omitting a stock dividend is permissible though not recommended.

> Common stock-holders obtain all net income in excess of expenses. Debt holders receive only contractual payments. If income falls, losses are borne by equity holders, while debt holders continue to receive interest.

An important corporate decision is how much debt and equity to raise. At the extremes are companies like Chock-Full-o'-Nuts, with virtually no debt, and companies like Texas International, with almost no equity compared to their debt. Most companies choose to have a debt

Table 6–1
Methods for Raising Equity Funds

Technique	Description
Sell common stock	Ownership of common stock allows the holder to elect the company's board of directors, the group responsible for overseeing the firm. Dividends may be paid but are not required. Each share represents an equal ownership percentage.
Sell preferred stock	Usually these shares do not vote in company elections, but normally dividends are paid. Sometimes these shares may be advantageously converted into common stock.
Sell warrants	A warrant is a long-term stock option. It gives the holder the right to buy common stock at a fixed price until a future date.
Issue rights	A right allows the holder to buy common stock at a discounted price. Rights are given to owners who may sell them to others.

Table 6–2
Methods for Obtaining Debt Funds

Technique	Description
Sell bonds	A bond is a corporate IOU. In exchange for lending the firm money, the lender receives periodic interest payments. Interest rates are usually fixed. Some bonds may be converted into common stock; some bonds are secured (collateralized) with real property like machines or real estate. The lender's money is returned at an appointed future time.
Obtain short-term loans	Usually received from a commercial lender for a term not to exceed one year but typically renewed. Often the loan carries a variable rate of interest below the current long-term interest rate.
Obtain trade credit	Money owed to suppliers, usually cost less financing, at least for a short period of time.

percentage equivalent to between 30 and 40 percent of total assets. The reason companies tend to avoid the near-zero down payment philosophy so popular in the real estate field is that prudent corporate management requires a safety net of equity funds to enable the firm to survive short-term losses. To understand this point better, let us pursue the real estate analogy. Suppose a bank allowed an investor to buy property with nothing down so that the bank lent all the funds used to make the purchase. Then suppose that in the first year, the property's expenses exceeded revenues. If the investor covered this loss, there would be no immediate problem. But if the investor lacked the funds to cover this loss or chose to walk away from the project, the bank's investment would be at risk. The property might have to be sold to another investor for less than the original mortgage value, leaving the bank with a capital loss. A similar situation could easily arise if any asset were purchased using no equity funds and all debt financing.

How much equity is prudent is a subjective decision. Two well-managed companies in the same business may choose quite different ratios of debt to equity based on legitimate motivational differences. For instance, a firm using more equity funds might be more concerned with the risk of failure, while a firm with greater debt financing seeks to increase the owner's financial return. In conducting our autopsies, it might be possible to say that one firm had too little equity since it failed or too much equity since its owners' earnings were insufficient. And yet without the power of hindsight, the manager's choices may have been sound and well thought out.

Comparing High Debt to High Equity

Suppose a firm needs $1 million to begin operating. It can sell common stock at $8 per share, it can sell bonds paying interest at 14 percent per

Table 6–3
Balance Sheet for a Company Needing $1 Million

	Assets			
Plan A:	Current Assets	$ 400,000	Debt	$ 200,000
Conservative	Noncurrent Assets	600,000	Equity	800,000
	Total	1,000,000	Total	1,000,000
Plan B:	Current Assets	$ 400,000	Debt	$ 800,000
Aggressive	Noncurrent Assets	600,000	Equity	200,000
	Total	1,000,000	Total	1,000,000

year, or both. How much money should it raise with stocks and how much with bonds? Two distinctly different financing plans are illustrated in table 6–3. With both plans, the firm raises $1 million, but in plan A it sells 100,000 shares of stock to raise $800,000 and sells $200,000 in bonds. Plan B has the firm raising $800,000 with a bond sale and selling 25,000 shares of stock to raise equity of $200,000. Two important differences between the plans must be highlighted:

1. There is four times as much debt in plan B as in plan A.
2. Four times as many shares are issued in plan A as in plan B.

Plan A is relatively more conservative since it raises little debt. Most of the $1 million is raised by selling ownership in the firm. Notice, however, that the firm is operationally the same with both plans, since the current asset–fixed asset split is not affected by the choice between stocks or bonds. This firm's operating leverage is the same with both plans.

Where diversity between the two plans is most noticeable is in the income statement prepared for a fictitious year in table 6–4. First notice that regardless of how many dollars of revenue are generated, $28,000 and $112,000 of interest must be paid with plan A and B, respectively. These amounts equal 14 percent (the annual percentage interest charge) multiplied by the dollar amount of bonds sold. Second, because operating leverage is independent of the financial plan, operating income is the same with plans A and B at every revenue level. Compare earnings per share (EPS) differences between the plans. When revenue is high, plan B provides a higher EPS, but when revenue is low, EPS is higher with plan A. In fact, the company loses $1.28 per share in the low revenue case with plan B.

	Plan A	Plan B
High revenue	$2.32	$5.92
Medium revenue	$1.47	2.52
Low revenue	$0.52	($1.28)

Table 6–4
Income Statement of a Firm Needing $1 Million

	Plan A	Plan B
High revenues		
Revenue	$750,000	$750,000
Operating cost	– 490,000	– 490,000
Operating profit	260,000	260,000
Interest	– 28,000	– 112,000
Net income	$232,000	$148,000
Earnings per share	$2.32	$5.92
Medium revenues		
Revenue	$625,000	$625,000
Operating cost	– 450,000	– 450,000
Operating profit	175,000	175,000
Interest	– 28,000	– 112,000
Net income	$147,000	$ 63,000
Earnings per share	$1.47	$2.52
Low revenues		
Revenue	$500,000	$500,000
Operating cost	– 410,000	– 410,000
Operating profit	80,000	80,000
Interest	– 28,000	– 112,000
Net income	$ 52,000	$(32,000)
Earnings per share	$0.52	($1.28)

Which plan is preferred? The answer depends on revenue. If revenue is high (low), then plan B (A) is better. Since future revenues are unknown, the correct choice is uncertain. Companies perform financial analysis to indicate under which circumstances each plan is best. A poor choice may turn a condor, a firm that might otherwise survive, into a dinosaur, a firm that will fail.

The best method for contrasting alternate financial plans is to calculate each plan's *financial leverage*. Like operating leverage, financial leverage is calculated as the percentage growth rate in EPS divided by the percentage growth rate in operating income. Table 6–5 works through financial leverage calculations for plans A and B. Financial leverage equals 1.19 in plan A and 2.78 in plan B. This means that when operating income (revenues less expenses excluding financing costs) increases by 1 percent, EPS rises by 1.19 percent in plan A and by 2.78 percent in plan B. When operating income falls, EPS declines by these same percentages. In fact, when revenue is $500,000, EPS is less than zero in plan B. High financial leverage is desirable when operating income is rising, but it harms EPS when operating income falls.

Table 6–5
Calculating Financial Leverage: Going from $625,000 to $750,000 in Revenue

	Plan A	Plan B
Change in earnings per share	$0.85	$3.40
Percentage change in earnings per share	57.8%	135.0%
Change in operating income	$85,000	$85,000
Percentage change in operating income	48.6%	48.6%
Financial leverage	1.19	2.78

Comparing Debt Levels across Firms

Although a perfect debt-to-equity ratio does not exist, techniques for comparing debt ratios across companies are still needed in order to classify firms into risk-of-failure categories. Notice, however, that bankruptcy occurs as a result of numerous causes, so it is possible for a firm in a low debt risk category to fail. For example, a tortoise might be a firm in a weak industry that has little debt. The tortoise's healthy financial condition might not keep it from failing should industry or product conditions worsen.

Table 6–6 lists five financial ratios commonly used to evaluate the degree of indebtedness. The last four of these ratios compare a concept from the asset side of the balance sheet to a concept on the liability side of the balance sheet. The idea is that assets represent value or worth, and liabilities show debt. By comparing worth to debt, a measure of financial health is found. For example, the quick ratio compares current assets to current liabilities. In most firms, this ratio is approximately equal to two; that is, firms tend to have nearly twice as many current assets (those assets convertible or converting into cash within a year) as they have current liabilities. One reason this ratio exceeds a unity value is that during times of financial crisis, current assets are often disposed of for less than their face value. For example, inventories may be sold to jobbers or discounters at prices below normal wholesale. Thus, a firm with a lower quick ratio has less liquidity.

Debt ratios indicate which firms use relatively more debt as compared to other firms and to themselves. Interfirm comparisons examine, for example, the debt ratios of a number of companies, all in the same industry. Firms with high degrees of financial leverage will also have higher debt ratios. A low debt ratio means greater contribution of funds by owners, higher book value per share, and less financial risk.

Intrafirm debt ratio comparisons, the repeated calculation of a firm's ratio for a series of years, quarters, or months, is perhaps the best

Table 6–6
Measures of Indebtedness

Concept	Terminology	Industry Average	Use
Debt/Equity[a]	Debt-to-equity ratio or debt ratio	0.50	A higher ratio indicates greater relative use of borrowed funds
Debt/Total assets[a]	Debt-to-asset ratio	0.30	In addition to indicating higher or lower use of borrowed funds, the ratio also indicates the proportion of total assets owned and the proportion borrowed
Long-term debt/Total assets	Long-term debt ratio	About 0.20	Compares future debt refunding or repayment needs to total assets
Current assets/Current liabilities	Quick ratio	2	Compares short-term liquidity to short-term need for funds
Total assets − total liability/Outstanding common shares	Book value per share	NM[b]	Provides a rough measure of liquidation value per share

[a]Debt includes all liabilities or, if one prefers, only long-term obligations.
[b]Not meaningful.

method for uncovering financial deterioration and an impending crisis. Financial policy changes, such as a decision to use more debt, may provide false signals of disaster and must be considered as the possible cause of an observed change in a financial ratio. Examples of intrafirm or time-series debt ratio comparisons are found in the two cases appearing in this chapter.

Deciding When There Is Too Much Debt

Knowing how much debt can be afforded is probably as vital for corporate survival as any other piece of information. Determination of the affordable level of debt is both a static and dynamic problem. The difference between static and dynamic analysis is that the former uses only historic, generally available information, while the latter incorporates data pertaining to the future. Corporate insiders are usually the only persons able to conduct a fully dynamic analysis since only they are privy to strategic plans. Although this section is written statically, it requires little modification to be performed dynamically within a company.

The two components in the debt affordability exercise are the company's cash inflows and cash outflows. As in the financial leverage discussion, we begin from the point where the firm has already calculated its operating income. There are known levels of sales, revenues, and cost of goods, exclusive of financing costs. At this stage, the cash flows without new debt financing can be calculated as follows:

Operating Cash Inflows	Financing Cash Outflows
New income	Debt interest payments
+ Depreciation	+ Preferred stock dividends
+ Other noncash expenses	+ Lease payments
Total cash inflow	Total cash outflow

Basically, inflows equal operating income plus noncash expenses (recorded expenses like depreciation which are not actually paid). Outflows equal financing costs.

Two facts are important to observe: (1) leasing and borrowing are treated as equivalents, and (2) no account is taken of lost opportunity value of the entrepreneur's invested capital. If leasing and borrowing are not viewed as identical, a firm would be able to make itself appear more solvent by leasing instead of buying equipment. The financial obligations of debt and long-term leases are the same, and thus the two are equivalent. Concerning lost opportunity value of capital, this important idea is captured by calculating the firm's return on equity (ROE), a measure of profitability. Between two otherwise identical firms, the one with the higher debt ratio has a higher ROE; it earns a greater percentage return on invested capital.

The affordability of debt is measured by dividing cash inflows by cash outflows:

$$\text{debt affordability measure} = \frac{\text{cash inflow}}{\text{cash outflow}}.$$

When the ratio is less than unity, there is too much debt since inflows are not sufficient to cover outflows. Even if the ratio is greater than unity, there may still be too much debt since the coverage of outflows by inflows may be too narrow; the risk of failure is significant if either revenues fall or expenses rise. Each business should know two sets of information concerning the debt affordability measure: (1) how its debt affordability measure has varied quarter by quarter over the past ten years and (2) how its competitors' debt affordability measures have varied over this period.

Armed with these facts, the firm will know when its financial condition begins to deteriorate.

Dome Petroleum   Condor ⟶ Dinosaur
Waiting Too Long to Sell Stock

Dome Petroleum, the second largest Canadian oil company with 1983 sales of nearly $2.6 billion (all dollar figures are reported in Canadian dollars worth about 76 cents U.S.), is in financial trouble. It has lost more than one quarter of a billion dollars in the last two years. Like International Harvester, were it not so large and so heavily in debt, it would now be bankrupt. A famous economist, John Maynard Keynes, is reported to have once said, "If you are a small borrower, you work for the bank; if you are a large borrower, the bank works for you." Dome is a good example of this paradox. With total debt of $6 billion as of March 1984, the company is almost too large to be pushed into bankruptcy. Instead of bankruptcy, Dome and its more than fifty lenders have agreed to reschedule debt and to raise more equity.

As of mid-1984, more than $1.9 billion of debt is overdue; lenders promised repayment by certain dates have not yet received their money. Although Dome has never missed paying lenders interest due them, lenders want their capital returned when promised. When repayment is not made on time, lenders quickly lose faith in a company and its managers. Any or all overdue lenders could file a petition of involuntary bankruptcy to force Dome to confront the repayment problem. The fact that lenders have not gone to court indicates their belief that they will be repaid more money by keeping Dome alive and by avoiding court costs.

How Dome got into this predicament can be described as getting lost with too little capital. First, management, led by founder John P. Gallagher, had aspirations of building a firm of awesome scale and profitability. Management almost exclusively used debt financing, preferring not to sell more shares of stock. For a while the strategy worked, as table 6–7 illustrates. Between 1974 and 1980, the price of the common stock rose by 1,750 percent. Dome's market value increased from $180 million to $3.5 billion. This growth in value was in large measure due to the use of financial leverage (Dome's degree of financial leverage equaled 1.27 for the period 1974 to 1980).

Gallagher's expansion plans for Dome were ambitious, risky, and built with mortar and bricks paid for with debt financing. Between 1974 and 1977, a conventional oil and gas drilling program allowed Dome to triple revenues ($171 million to $521 million) and almost quadruple profits ($28 million to $104 million), and it forced Dome to nearly quintuple

Table 6–7
Dome Petroleum Data

	Number of Common Shares (millions)	Price of Common Shares	Long-Term Debt (millions of dollars)	Total Debt (millions of dollars)	Debt Ratio
1974	224.99	$ 0.80			
1975	225.02	1.60			
1976	242.29	2.00			
1977	243.05	2.50			
1978	244.61	4.00	$ 599.1	$ 825.6	1.21
1979	246.26	10.00	1,362.8	1,712.5	1.54
1980	248.26	14.00	2,705.4	3,190.0	2.28
1981	250.06	14.00	6,394.5	7,472.5	6.27
1982	257.40	2.90	6,521.1	8,026.6	9.54
1983	267.89	3.00	5,987.3	7,511.6	NC[a]

[a]Not calculable.

long-term debt ($111 million to $521 million). Although hyperaccelerated, the growth was manageable.

The strategy became more adventuresome in 1977. Gold mines, shipbuilding, pipelines, and dispersed oil properties were acquired. By themselves, these purchases might have benefited Dome, but when coupled with two other ventures, the debt burden became too great. First, Gallagher looked to the Arctic Circle for major oil deposits. Although deposits were in fact found, the area is so inhospitable and environmentally pristine that even 100 million barrel oil reserves (in New York harbor worth over $3 billion) may not be economically exploitable. Someday this investment may pay off, but for now it is a financial albatross on Dome's neck.

Second, in 1981, Dome coveted Conoco's Canadian oil holdings. After making a tender offer for Conoco stock, which Conoco resisted, a compromise was arranged with Dome trading Conoco stock for Conoco land. That transaction cost Dome approximately $1.7 billion. When oil prices were high and rising, this was a sound investment. Now the deal seems less fortuitous.

Beginning in 1980, the debt affordability measure began to fall, indicating that the debt was getting harder to support. Table 6–8 lists the debt affordability measures for 1978 through 1983. By 1981, the measure was just a bit greater than 1.00, and in 1982, at 0.09, it rang an impending disaster bell. By then it was too late. Dome had $1.7 billion in debt come due in 1982. It was unable to repay these funds. A crisis had been reached. A plan of reorganization had to be developed. Also, as is often true in a crisis, a new management team was put in place. The new

Table 6–8
Dome Petroleum: Debt Affordability Measure
(millions of dollars)

	Cash Outflows	Cash Inflows	Debt Affordability
1978	$ 120.1	$ 365.1	$3.04
1979	215.3	753.3	3.50
1980	442.8	869.4	1.96
1981	863.0	916.8	1.06
1982	4,682.5	443.9	0.09
1983	1,263.6	(384.0)	NC[a]

[a]Not calculable because of negative cash inflows.

president, J. Howard MacDonald, was hired away from the Royal Dutch/
Shell Group. His assessment of Dome was straightforward: "[Dome had
been] buying everything in sight and doing it on debt, a hell of a risk."[1]
Although new managers may correctly perceive a firm's difficulties, how
to overcome them may not be so obvious. Dome needed more equity.
Equity is easiest to raise at precisely the time when current owners are
reluctant to share ownership with new stockholders. Once a firm en-
counters financial difficulties, common stock is no longer easy to sell.
In fact, it may be impossible.

McDonald has articulated his plans: "The easy thing to do would be
to give up and sit on your hands. [Dome intends] . . . to persevere."[2] His
plan seems to consist of five parts:

1. Sell off assets to accumulate cash. Nearly $1 billion in assets has
   been sold since the change in management.
2. Sell new equity. Dome is attempting to sell 100 million common
   shares and 50 million warrants. If successful, this would bring in up-
   wards of $300 million.
3. Obtain a delay in the repayment schedule. The refinancing agreement, which is contingent on the equity sale, delays repayment of
   debt for twelve years.
4. Obtain new bank credit. If the refinancing plan goes through, $352
   million in new credits will be forthcoming.
5. Develop a workable business plan. The company has adopted a
   more cautious approach. For example, future exploration in the Arctic will be paid for by partners in joint ventures.

Only the future will tell if this plan works. But these five steps constitute
a good revitalization outline for any company finding itself lost with too
little capital.

Of the five steps, the fifth is without question the most important since it creates the foundation on which old and new creditors must find assurances of future solvency. New equity can never be raised unless investors perceive that a prosperous company will eventually emerge. It is within the business plan that these hopes are to be sought.

In deciding whether new managers are needed, the most salient question may be this: can the current managers (the architects of the existing plan) see the future through new eyes, or will they insist on trying to make the old plan work? If they prefer to keep working with the old plan, it may be necessary to seek a new team.

Computer Devices   Eagle ⟶ Dinosaur
The Case of David against Goliath

On October 31, 1983, Computer Devices filed for protection under Chapter 11 of the bankruptcy code. So ended a plan to turn a small but profitable high-technology company into a force on the leading edge of technology. Had Computer Devices not attempted to grow, probably it would have had an ample capital and equity base to survive; however, it got lost with too little capital when it tried to grow.

Computer Devices was a successful computer terminal manufacturer. Its portable terminal products set an industry standard and generated ample profits. By 1981, however, sales growth slowed, and the firm needed a new product to regain momentum. Table 6–9 highlights the financial results leading up to 1981. Notice two important facts in the table: (1) the company was profitable, and (2) its ratio of debt to total assets in 1981, 22 percent was not a cause for concern. For example, Prime Computer, a successful computer company in 1983, had a ratio

Table 6–9
Computer Devices' Financial Summary
(thousands of dollars)

	1979	1980	1981
Total revenue	$17,661	$20,091	$19,143
Net income	1,169	1,182	1,228
Earnings per share	0.48	0.42	0.44
Total assets		18,203	17,676
Total stockholders' equity		11,266	12,500
Total debt[a]		5,678	3,936

[a]The missing item, deferred income taxes, is not relevant.

of debt to total assets of 25 percent. Thus, as 1981 ended, Computer Devices could look back on the three years since its creation (as a result of a merger with TechVen Association, Inc.) with pride and a feeling of accomplishment.

The next twenty-two months, however, was a time of great expectation and eventual collapse. The strategy that eventually led to Computer Device's failure—to enter the personal computer market—could be described in one of two ways. The optimistic view says that a company with a strong base of customers should have been able to gain a healthy share of the burgeoning personal computer (PC) market by offering a superior product. The other view, one familiar to everyone, is that it takes money to make money.

By entering the PC market, Computer Devices was taking on IBM. Very few companies have ever done that and survived. The list of unsuccessful efforts to compete with IBM is long and includes such corporate names as RCA and General Electric. In order to win in a battle with Goliath, David must have everything going for him. A single shortcoming is enough to result in disaster. Compter Devices came close to winning, but it lacked enough capital to compete with giants and thus lost out.

Each business possesses product and financial characteristics that may be either healthy or weak. Four types of businesses are identified by interacting product and financial characteristics: eagles, tortoises, condors, and dinosaurs. Computer Devices can actually be categorized in two locations in the business classification matrix in table 1–1 depending on its choice of strategies. Had the firm chosen only to update the computer terminal products responsible for its past successes, it would be classfied as a small eagle, a firm destined for prosperity. After all, as table 6–10 shows, profits were positive and steady through 1981, and according to industry surveys, its products were very highly rated versus the competition.

By adopting a new products strategy instead, the company must be reclassified in the matrix at best as a condor, a company with a tendency to survive. As with all other tendencies or probabilities, sometimes they do not hold true, and their opposites occur. That is, condors may fail, as did Computer Devices.

It is worthwhile considering why Computer Devices became a condor when it chose to introduce its own version of the PC. First, consider the product. The DOT, Computer Device's PC, was an entry into the portable PC market that offered many improvements over existing products. It has a built-in printer (the same as that used in the company's terminals), a good keyboard, clear display, and communications capabilities. Technical experts gave the DOT high marks. In other words, as the strategy was being implemented, the product was healthy.

Table 6–10
Computer Devices' Quarterly Profits and Equity, 1982 and 1983
(millions of dollars)

	1982				1983			
	1st Quarter	2nd Quarter	3rd Quarter	4th Quarter	1st Quarter	2nd Quarter	3rd Quarter	4th Quarter
Profits	$0.16	$0.003	$(0.70)	$(4.40)	$(1.20)	$(3.90)	$(6.50)	$(8.90)
Stockholders' equity	12.80	12.80	12.10	7.70	6.50	2.60	—[a]	(1.50)

[a]In July, the company sold 1 million shares of common stock, new equity, for $11.25 per share, raising equity by $11.3 million. Thus, equity of $7.1 million really belongs in this quarter, but note, this $7.1 million equals $2.6 million (equity in 83:2) plus $11.3 million (the new equity), minus $6.5 million (the loss in 1983, the 3rd quarter).

To bring a product such as the DOT to market requires a major investment in research and development, production capability, distribution networks, and marketing. As of the end of 1981, Computer Devices was not overendowed with financial resources. It had working capital (current assets minus current liabilities) of $4.3 million and a modest level of debt relative to equity: $5.2 million versus $12.5. In short, Computer Devices was in a weak financial condition considering its plans. It was a condor, a financially weak firm with a healthy product. The company's finances would have been healthy had it remained exclusively in its original business.

In order to bring the DOT to market and to carry out its continuing businesses in 1982, Computer Devices raised its debt level to $12.9 million, 150 percent over the previous year. Most of the new funds, almost $6 million, was raised through bank loans, with the remaining funds obtained as credit from suppliers (accounts payable). One result of higher debt levels is increased interest expense. But this constitutes a problem only when the new assets for which the funds are borrowed are either wasted or misused; that is, problems develop only if the new assets fail to generate sufficient profits to pay the interest costs.

A second result of higher debt levels is that it becomes difficult to increase debt further. There is a practical level of debt beyond which any company, or for that matter any person, cannot go. Lenders insist on equity dollars to protect debt dollars. When the ratio of debt to equity passes a certain point, further debt is either impossible or else very expensive to obtain.

With the new debt obtained in 1982, Computer Devices had come close to reaching its debt limit. Without a further increase in equity, obtained by selling new stock, bankers would hesitate before authorizing further debt increases. Having practically reached its debt limit would not necessarily have been problematic for Computer Devices had the DOT begun to generate profits. Instead the DOT became a drain on the company.

Let's pick up the story as 1982 begins. First, a new terminal product announced by Computer Devices midway through 1981 and expected to be in production by the second quarter of 1982 fell way behind schedule. Although production did finally commence in December 1982, the delay hurt the company in three ways: higher engineering and research costs, lost sales and lost profits, and a loss in confidence of suppliers, creditors, bankers, and customers.

The second problem surfacing in 1982 was the higher than expected cost of bringing the DOT to market. The company had to hire new personnel, to upgrade the manufacturing facility, and to install new equipment. Overall engineering and research costs nearly tripled over the previous year. As a result, Computer Devices lost nearly $5 million in 1982, with all of the loss occurring in the last half of the year. Since losses reduce stockholders' equity, the company ended 1982 with a worse ratio of debt to equity. To correct this situation, it sold 1 million new shares of stock in July 1983, raising $11 million of equity.

As the year closed, there was a hint of better days to come. Orders were received for the purchase of nearly 5,000 DOTs in each of the next two years. To accommodate these and other expected orders, the firm expanded its production capability for the DOT to a level of several thousand units per month. With the market for portable PCs estimated to be 2 million units per year, the company was proceeding cautiously. After all, it must have reasoned, it was building a superior product and had built its operating capability to a level requiring a market share (the proportion of the total market held) of only 1.2 percent. If ninety-nine out of every one hundred PCs expected to be sold in 1983 were acquired from competitors and only one out of one hundred was purchased from Computer Devices, the firm would be a success.

Although it is usually difficult to explain why a superior product fails, in the DOT's case, there is a simple explanation: the DOT was not IBM-compatible. As is becoming clearer and clearer each day, it is virtually impossible to compete in the PC market unless the product is IBM-compatible. Although the reasons for their failure were not exactly the same as those for Computer Devices, other firms that tried and failed to gain a position in this market include Eagle Computer, Columbia Data, Gavilan Computer, Osborne Computer, and Franklin Computer. By now, the list is surely longer.

The market signaled a rejection of the DOT by the rapid decline in orders for the product. In each of the four months preceding bankruptcy filing, the company received orders for approximately fifty machines a month. Manufacturing capacity exceeded several thousand units a month. With high operating costs and low product revenues, losses were inevitable. Table 6–10 lists quarterly 1982 and 1983 profits and losses.

By at least the second quarter of 1983, the disastrous consequences of not being IBM-compatible were clear. Management had two alternatives:

1. Shut down the company, liquidate assets, and distribute the excess of asset value over liabilities to shareholders.
2. Raise new capital by an equity offering and produce an IBM-compatible version of the DOT.

The company adopted choice 2.

The idea of raising new capital to support only old products and dropping the DOT was probably not viable since it would have been difficult to sell equity in a company with an old product and a failed idea. Similarly, the idea of raising funds from banks or other traditional lenders was tried at this time, but the requests were refused, though banks did advance limited funds.

Using the funds obtained in the equity offering, the company pursued the DOT II, the IBM-compatible version of its personal computer. But before the product could be brought to market, funds expired, and the company filed bankruptcy papers. Even after the Chapter 11 filing, however, the company intended to pursue the DOT II as it tried to interest new investors or to develop a corporate acquisition. Eventually a non-exclusive license was granted to another company (believed to be Prime Computer) for $200,000 for information gathered in the DOT project.

How important is equity? Sometimes a firm may survive forever with little equity. In other cases, failure results from a shortage of equity. Had Computer Devices begun with more capital, it might have self-financed the DOT II, brought an IBM-compatible product to market, and today have been a household name. The lesson in this failure should be clear: since the cost of excess capital is much less than the cost of insufficient capital, always err to the low side of the debt-to-equity choice.

Synopsis

If you allowed a new partner to join your successful business, you would have to split all profits in two: half for you and half for your partner. Adding a third partner would reduce even further your share of the profits. It is this requirement of equity that encourages so many companies to emphasize debt financing.

Although there are several good reasons for using debt financing, there is one major disadvantage: future alternatives are limited. Dome discovered this problem too late. Had Dome sold equity instead of some debt, its interest burden would have been reduced. By the time Dome chose to sell stock, the value of its common stock was far below previous levels, and thus the stock sale had less value.

Equity is owners' capital, money paid in exchange for ownership. Owners do not receive interest payments. Thus, firms using more equity pay less interest than firms using debt. As illustrated in the Computer Devices case, however, equity serves a second important purpose: a buffer against failure. Companies with sizable net worth or owners' equity can survive even if they make costly mistakes. A firm with limited equity is allowed fewer mistakes.

7
Getting Pinched by Short-Term Debt

All other things being equal, borrowers prefer a longer repayment schedule, and lenders prefer a shorter wait for the return of their money. Financial and economic writers call this well-known observation a *liquidity preference*. That is, despite the fact that more interest is owed or earned the longer the life of a loan, borrowers want the use of other people's money for as much time as possible, and lenders would almost rather that the money never left their sight at all.

Liquidity refers to the ease and cost of converting assets into cash. Being liquid is advantageous; however, total liquidity—holding all assets as cash—is costly since capital has an opportunity value. If all the assets are converted into cash, investors are not earning any interest on their wealth. Thus, in exchange for earning interest, investors endure a little risk. When risk increases, more interest is demanded. Thus, you would expect to pay (or receive) a higher rate of interest for a longer-term loan since it is more risky.

Interest for Risk: The Yield Curve

The amount of extra interest that "should" be charged to lengthen a loan's term by one more year is neither fixed nor certain. Usually to lengthen a one-year loan to five or six years requires about 1 to 2 percent extra annual interest, and an extra five years (for a total of ten years) might cost an additional 1 percent in annual interest. The graphical representation of all loan terms and corresponding interest rates is called the *yield curve* and is depicted in figure 7–1. Notice that longer-term loans usually pay higher rates of interest.

Interest rates are set by market forces. Lenders and borrowers come to market seeking an exchange. Only those participants willing to exchange at market rates actually conduct business. As shown in figure 7–2, the interest rate is determined by the intersection of the supply and demand for money. The market rate is the only rate that can clear the market. *Market clearing* means that everyone willing to participate

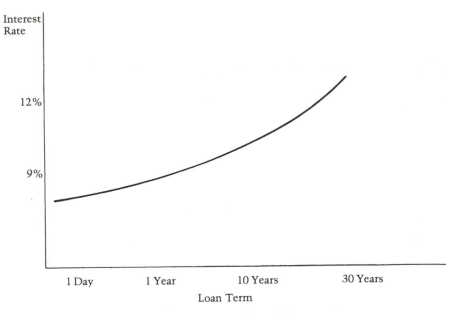

Figure 7–1. Typical Yield Curve

(that is, lend or borrow) at that rate can and does. Thus, the only lenders not lending are those insisting on being paid a higher rate. And the only borrowers not borrowing are those refusing to pay rates as high as the market is signaling.

Interest rates motivate borrowers and lenders to engage in an exchange. In a market system, discrimination between people occurs on the basis of their willingness to pay or receive the rate set by the market. Other less desirable means of discrimination, such as on the basis of race, sex, or national origin, are usually kept out of the marketplace by economic forces. The marketplace is blind to everything but money. As Karl Marx once said, "The capitalists will race each other to the gallows to sell the hangman a rope."

The market must determine an infinite number of interest rates simultaneously: a one hour rate (for people wanting to exchange money for one hour), a one day rate, a one year rate, a one century rate, and all rates in between. The yield curve in figure 7–1 summarizes this plenitude of rates and describes how much extra interest must be paid to compensate for the additional risk associated with longer-term loans.

Sometimes the yield curve assumes a perverse shape, as depicted in figure 7–3. The only instances of upside-down yield curves in the last half-century were during 1979, 1981, and 1982. At each of these times,

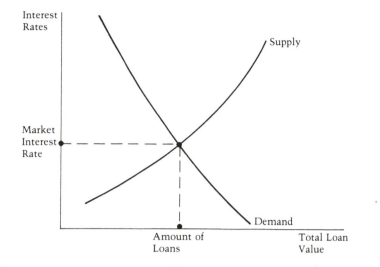

Figure 7–2. Determination of Interest Rates by Market Forces

short-term rates, most notably the prime rate of interest, rose to the vicinity of 20 percent interest per year. Although longer-term interest rates also increased, the increase in short rates outweighed the longer-term rate rise, producing the perverse shape. Two conclusions, one obvious and one more esoteric, are drawn from a perverse yield curve:

1. Short-term loans at such times are more expensive (they require higher interest payments) than longer-term loans.
2. The market is forecasting that interest rates will begin to decline.

If long-term rates are lower than short-term rates, most cost-conscious executives will borrow long-term money. An executive who believes all interest rates are about to fall, however, may borrow short-term money now and hope to replace it later with long-term money. If rates do not fall, the borrower may get pinched by short-term debt.

Regarding the forecast of future interest rates derivable from the slope (shape) of the yield curve, the simplest rule is to treat the curve like an arrow. When the yield curve is almost flat (for example, with a 1 percent increase for five-year notes versus one year notes and an additional 1 percent increase out to ten years), the forecast is for steady rates. In other words, the market is requiring borrowers to compensate lenders for their liquidity risk and for nothing else. By contrast, a steep yield curve, when the arrow is pointing upward, means that to increase loan terms by five or ten years takes more than just a 2 percent interest pre-

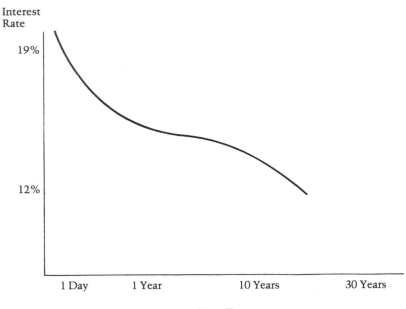

Figure 7–3. Perverse Yield Curve

mium. Sometimes a rate premium of 4 to 6 percent is required. The extra premium is paid to cover a second risk: higher future rates. Finally, when the yield curve arrow is pointing down, the extra interest rate premium is less than zero. This means that lenders not only see no risk of higher future rates but in fact are scurrying to lock in high long-term rates. When more long-term loanable money is available, long-term rates decline, and the risk premium is negative.

Ten Steps to Bankruptcy

High short-term interest rates do not by themselves cause bankruptcies. Short-term rates tend to induce failure only when the following steps are taken:

1. The borrowing firm needs additional funds.
2. The firm chooses increased debt, as opposed to more equity, to raise the funds.
3. Management expects interest rates to fall in the near future.
4. Management decides not to postpone the planned investment until rates decline.

5. Short-term debt is obtained. A future refinancing is planned when interest rates fall.
6. Interest rates rise, but management still foresees lower future rates, so debt is refinanced, again using short-term money.
7. Step 6 occurs a number of times.
8. Eventually the interest cost on the debt leads to income losses and a liquidity crisis.
9. Credit is lost, and the debt cannot be refinanced.
10. The firm goes bankrupt.

In other words, bankruptcy may result if management decides to speculate on lower future interest rates. Countless times, management's interest rate guess is correct, and rates do drop. In that case, the gamble will lead to higher future profits since interest costs are lower than would otherwise be the case. When management is wrong, however, profits may be lower, or bankruptcy may result.

Given the range of consequences from interest rate speculation, it hardly seems appropriate for companies to ever engage in the practice. Yet many businesses attempt to beat the financial system and wind up getting pinched by short-term debt.

Before we become overcritical of business leaders, let us consider how often individuals yield to the temptation of lower short-term interest rates when they buy assets such as homes or condominiums with variable-rate mortgages. It has been reported that as many as 60 percent of all recent mortgages were variable, with higher interest rates a possibility or else with a balloon payment requirement. In either event, if future interest rates rise, many of these buyers may lose their dwellings. Why do people engage in this gamble? In some cases, the answer is simple: without the lower rate offered with a variable mortgage, the purchaser could never afford the unit. Maybe for these individuals, the speculation is acceptable; however, anyone gambling on a variable-rate mortgage should be pretty confident of future trends or else should read the Wickes case, below.

Wickes   Tortoise ⟶ Dinosaur

Besides the failure of the Penn Central Transportation in 1970, the bankruptcy filing on April 24, 1982, by Wickes was the largest corporate failure in U.S. business history. The major reason for the company's failure appears to be its heavy reliance on short-term debt. When interest rates increased, the company failed.

Higher interest rates hurt Wickes in two ways. First, Wickes operated in interest-sensitive businesses (lumber, building supplies, and furniture). When interest rates rose, business activity in these sectors slumped, and Wickes's sales and profits fell. Without adequate profits or cash flow, the firm was vulnerable and got caught in a product bankruptcy trap. Second, Wickes relied too heavily on short-term debt. Rising interest rates increased the interest burden, leading to a liquidity crisis and eventually causing the firm's failure.

Wickes's corporate beginnings go back as far as the mid-nineteenth century. By 1980 it was a conglomerate with sales in excess of $2 billion, annual profits of nearly $40 million, and stockholders' equity of almost $280 million, or $25.69 per share. The stock market was not overly impressed with Wickes, however, despite a book value in excess of $25.00 per share, the stock traded between $13.62 and $17.25 per share in 1980. That is, the market chose to value the company at about 60 percent of book value.

There are three typical reasons why a company's stocks might trade at less than book value:

1. The balance sheet overstates the true value of the company's assets and hence its book value too.
2. Management is considered to be incapable of properly directing assets.
3. The firm is subject to abnormally high risks (for example, most of its assets may be in foreign countries or its business might depend on new, untested technologies).

In the Wickes case, all three explanations probably apply to some degree.

Although the best strategy for overcoming stock market undervaluation is to improve the performance of assets already owned, many companies instead attempt to increase stock values by giving the impression of growth by merging or acquiring other companies. Sometimes this strategy works—usually when the acquired company either fits nicely with the acquiring company or the acquired company is actually a better company (for example, a condor acquiring a small eagle). Wickes chose to follow this approach. The gambit did not work.

In August 1980, Wickes acquired Gambles-Skogmo Inc., a retailer of approximately equal size to Wickes itself. It is doubtful that Gambles was acquired because it fit well with Wickes; there was little overlap between the products or regions served by the two companies. Thus, the merger probably would not decrease average costs or increase return on investment. Neither does Gambles appear to have been a better company than Wickes, as we can see from the profit margin comparison in table 7–1.

Table 7–1
Wickes and Gambles-Skogmo: Profit Margin Comparison

	Wickes	*Gambles-Skogmo*
1979	0.018	0.012
1980	0.019	0.015

A remark made by Wickes's chairman, E.L. McNeeley, just after the merger, "We haven't really noodled out what we are going to do," suggests that, more than anything else, the only preconceived objective for this merger was for Wickes to grow.[1]

In terms of products, a growth-for-growth's-sake acquisition is bad strategy. It can only be characterized as weak. Even if Wickes had healthy products prior to acquiring Gambles, it became weaker afterward. Yet the company did not need to fail. Failure was guaranteed by a weak financial plan. The overuse of short-term debt to pay the acquisition bill turned Wickes into a dinosaur.

On paper, Wickes appears to have struck a good deal. Table 7–2 describes, using approximate values, the type of financial analysis that

Table 7–2
Analysis of the Gambles-Skogmo Aquisition

Cost to Wickes

Pay out $33.00 for each of 4.2
million Gambles-Skogmo shares .... $138.60 million

Give 0.75 share of Wickes Companies
in exchange for each share of
Gambles-Skogmo .... $ 47.25 million

    Total dollar cost .... $185.85 million

Assume Gambles-Skogmo's debt .... $ 1.00 billion

Benefit to Wickes

Gambles-Skogmo's cash flow, based
on 1980 (figure calculated after
paying interest on Gambles-Skogmo's
debt) .... $ 52.48 million

Net benefit

= $52.48 million − opportunity cost of the invested $185.85 million

= $52.48 million − ($185.85 million) × (11%)[a]

= $52.48 million − $20.44 million

= $32.04 million

[a]The prime rate in August 1980.

probably justified the acquisition. Wickes paid approximately $185 million for Gambles and in addition took on (agreed to repay) almost $1 billion in existing Gambles debt. While a $1 billion debt is sizable, in the year prior to the acquisition, Gambles had an after-interest-payment cash flow (net profit plus depreciation) of more than $52 million. Thus the debt did not seem unmanageable. However, Wickes's net gain on the acquisition would be less than the $52 million since its invested $185 million had an opportunity value of approximately $20 million in 1980. Yet the acquisition seemed perfect. Wickes would double in sales and assets and would increase true profits by almost $32 million per year. The plan failed to work.

Wickes's failure is best explained by examining table 7–3 and inspecting Wickes short-term debt before and after the acquisition. The acquisition took place in August 1980 between the 1980 and 1981 fiscal years. The increase in Wickes's short-term debt in 1981 from 1980 ($132.9 million) is almost exactly equal to the actual cash outflow ($138.6 million) paid in the acquisition (see table 7–2). Thus Wickes appears to have financed the acquisition entirely using short-term bank debt.

In the time period preceding the acquisition, the United States experienced unprecedented inflation that propelled interest rates skyward. Table 7–3 shows that short-term interest rates were moving upward. Management must have felt that rates would soon decline. Since the interest savings for each 1 percentage point decline in rates for $135 million owed is $1⅓ million per year, or in Wickes case $0.09 per share, the company arguably decided to risk its future on an interest rate speculation. In retrospect, it was a bad choice.

Calendar year 1981 (January to December 1981) was hard on the economy but harder still on Wickes. High interest rates led to an economic slowdown as construction activity and the sale of durable goods declined precipitously. The portion of Wickes's sales in the construction and home furnishings markets followed the economy downward. The company's remaining sales, mostly in the retail sector, were hurt by high

Table 7–3
Wickes's Short-Term Debt, Year Ending January 31
(millions of dollars)

	1978	1979	1980	1981	1982
Short-term debt	$33.00	$21.60	$102.20	$235.10	$648.90
Average prime interest rate	9.0%	12.7%	15.3%	18.9%	14.9%
Interest due on short-term debt	$2.97	$2.74	$15.64	$44.43	$96.70

Table 7–4
Wickes's Income Statement, As of January 30
(millions of dollars)

	1978	1979	1980	1981	1982	1983
Sales	$1,487.9	$1,910.1	$2,095.2	$2,876.9	$3,517.2	$2,638.2
Interest	24.0	32.7	38.5	117.2	172.5	50.1
Store Closing					200.1	42.1
Reserve write-off						52.2
Asset disposal loss				4.1	38.5	75.0
Net income	28.8	34.4	39.7	8.3	(258.3)	(248.7)

unemployment and the decline in personal disposable income. Finally, Wickes's interest expense exploded upward because of high rates. Wickes was no longer profitable.

Table 7–4 summarizes Wickes's income statement over this period. The acquisition occurred between the 1980 and 1981 fiscal years. Prior to the acquisition, Wickes was relatively healthy; afterward it was not. Why did earnings fall off? In 1981, the reason is total interest expense. Wickes paid over 200 percent more interest in fiscal year 1981 than in 1980: $117.2 million versus $38.5 million. The higher expense is mostly due to the increasing interest rates. When the acquisition took place in August 1980, the prime interest rate was 11.5 percent. By December 1980, the prime rate hit 21.5 percent and hovered in this range until December 1981, when it fell to 15.75 percent. By then the damage was done.

In fiscal year 1981, Wickes earned a small profit of $8.3 million only because the high debt began midyear (in August) and interest rates did not spurt up until late in the year (November and December 1980). Fiscal year

Table 7–5
Wickes's Debt

Class	Name	Type of Debt	Amount[a]
1	Priority	Wages, taxes	$25.0 million
2	Senior	Trade debt, notes, debentures, and other senior debt	$929.0 million
3	Subordinated	Subordinated debentures, income notes, convertibles	$328.9 million
4	Preferred stock	Stock	402,980 shares
5	Common stock	Stock	14,385,439 shares

Note: Table based on Wickes's court filing dated June 22, 1984.
[a]Prior to proposing this plan, the company settled $350 million of indebtedness.

Table 7–6
Wickes's Reorganization Plan

Class	Cash (millions)	Two-Year Notes	Nine-Year Debenture (@ 12%)	Twenty-Year Debenture (@ 8.75%)
Priority	$25.0			
Senior	$296.4	$153.1	$242.6	
Subordinated	$1.6	$15.8		$150.0
Preferred				
Common				

[a]Reflect market values, not book values. The two-year notes had a value of $165.1 million, the nine-year debentures had a value of $223.2 million, and the twenty-year notes had a value of $79.4 million. The stock was valued at about $4.60 per share inclusive of the warrants.

[b]Not meaningful.

Fiscal year 1982 (February 1981–January 1982) was many times worse than 1981 for Wickes because 1982 was a full year of high debt and high interest rates. In 1982, Wickes lost more than a quarter of a billion dollars. It lost a similar amount in 1983 as well. The 1982 loss nearly wiped out the stockholders' equity of $294.5 million that Wickes began with in 1982. The 1983 loss left Wickes with an accumulated deficit in stockholders' equity of $230 million. This deficit means that after losing nearly half a billion dollars in just two years, Wickes had gone through all the monies shareholders had ever invested in Wickes, as well as all the profits Wickes had retained over the previous century.

Most of Wickes's two-year losses—$412 million out of $507 million —resulted from store closings, asset write-offs, and asset disposal. These losses represent the dollars lost in shutting down businesses that had no future potential. Since many of the written-off assets had belonged to Gambles, it is also reasonable to conclude that Wickes had wasted assets and therefore failed.

By January 1982, Wickes had short-term bank borrowings of $575 million and another $73.6 million in long-term debt that was maturing. Its line of credit held $72.5 million in unborrowed funds; however, in a year-end review, the banks lowered the credit line to $580.9 million, which exactly equaled Wickes short-term debt on that date, February 16, 1982. The message conveyed from the banks by this action was that Wickes was on its own. Trade creditors took similar actions, making it difficult for Wickes to acquire goods on credit. As a result, nine weeks after the banks' actions, Wickes failed.

Why would bankers put a company into a position almost guaranteeing failure? From the banks' perspective, Wickes had already failed; it

Shares of Stock	Number of Warrants	Value as Percentage of Claim	
		Book	Market[a]
		100.0%	100.0%
51,404,000 shares	959,000	100.0%	97.5%
27,716,000 shares	7,193,000	90.0%	68.8%
2,400,000 shares		NM[b]	NM[b]
14,385,439 shares	2,877,000	15.0%	15.0%

must have seemed to be a bottomless pit. No matter how much money they lent, Wickes wanted more. In 1982 alone, Wickes's bank debt had almost tripled. Moreover, much of the nearly $350 million increase in bank loans in 1982 was probably really interest owed that Wickes was unable to pay. The banks must have believed they were cutting their losses.

When Wickes filed its reorganization petition, it had over $1.6 billion in liabilities subject to settlement. There were fewer dollars of assets, based on book values, available to pay off these liabilities. Thus, certain debt or equity holders would receive less than full redemption on their claims.

Essentially the priority of claims in a Chapter 11 reorganization is based on creditor seniority. In finance, seniority has little to do with when the debt was first incurred; instead it concerns the contractual agreement among the creditor, debtor, and previous creditors in regard to who will get paid off first. Five classes of Wickes creditors were identified. Table 7–5 lists the five creditor classes and the amount of their claims. Table 7–6 describes for each creditor class the allocation of cash, debt, and stock proposed in the June 22, 1984, reorganization plan.

Claimants higher up on the priority schedule received greater value in the reorganization plan as a percentage of their claim. For example, class 1 in the priority schedule received a 100 percent allocation. By contrast, class 3, subordinated debt, received a 90 percent allocation based on book values; however, this allocation is only 68 percent when market (true) values are used since the market will discount Wickes's new debt.

Wickes's common stockholders will be allowed to keep their shares and will be given warrants to purchase one new share for every five shares owned; however, since an additional 81.5 million shares are being issued to other creditors, the ownership of common stockholders is diluted to merely 15 percent of the company. Thus, they suffer the greatest percentage loss of all claimants.

While it is true that common shareholders generally lose the most when a company files a Chapter 11 reorganization petition under the federal bankruptcy code, it is also true that in liquidation (Chapter 7 of the federal bankruptcy code) stockholders often receive nothing. In the Wickes case, company officials contend that in a liquidation, only $575 million to $675 million would have been received to cover the $1.6 billion debt. Shareholders would get nothing. The reorganization produced an additional $437 million since the 95 million shares to be issued each has a value of approximately $4.60.

Creditors do not always prefer reorganization to liquidation. The deciding element is which choice gives them the most dollars. A reorganization that produces a new dinosaur, a company destined to fail, will ultimately cost creditors money since some of their settlement is either in the form of common stock or debt in the new company, which is not collectible for some years to come.

Synopsis

Of the five bankruptcy traps detailed in previous chapters, business people are most vulnerable to getting pinched by short-term debt. Prior to 1979, long-term interest rates were always higher than short-term rates. Thus, managers safely chose the loan maturity with the lowest interest rate and both reduced costs and avoided unnecessary risks.

Since 1979, there have been at least three periods with perverse yield curves. Long-term rates lower than short-term rates (the perverse shape) appear whenever high inflation seems about to be beaten. At these times, managers looking for the lowest rates would borrow long term; however, a manager believing that all interest rates are about to fall might adopt another strategy of immediate short-term borrowing, followed eventually by long-term borrowing. The cost of adopting this strategy is a higher failure risk. Most firms engaging in this practice will survive because interest rates will actually fall. But some firms will fail when all rates continue upward after the company has accepted a short-term loan.

8
Detecting Future Bankruptcies

Does bankruptcy generate any benefits? To be sure, bankruptcy provides employment to thousands of attorneys, accountants, financial managers, stress counselors, and other professionals whose livelihoods are based on assisting failed companies and their employees. But everyone else associated with a bankruptcy is worse off than if the failure had been avoided. For that reason, learning to detect impending bankruptcies is a responsibility shared by managers, investors, and employees alike.

Equity investors normally suffer the greatest financial loss in a bankruptcy since their claims are at the bottom of the priority schedule. It may be true that investing in already bankrupt companies can be a good financial strategy, but the investments of original investors who took equity positions prior to the onset of failure are certainly almost never recovered. If this were not true, healthy companies would go bankrupt in order to increase the value of their shareholders' wealth, and this, of course, never happens.

Debt holders also lose when companies fail. Sometimes, when analysts examine a case like Wickes where senior debt holders recover dollar for dollar the value of their claims, they mistakenly assert that secured debtors do not share in the bankruptcy's financial consequences. This impression needs to be corrected. Even in these cases, debt holders are harmed in two ways. First, they suffer an opportunity loss. Over two and a half years will have elapsed between Wickes's Chapter 11 petition and the distribution of new securities to claimants. During the interim, the investors' funds are unavailable and are not earning interest. On average, reorganizations take about two years, though larger failures may extend the process length to nine or ten years.[1] Wickes's managers acknowledged working to limit the reorganization period.

Second, debt holders generally prefer steady cash flows (interest) to capital appreciation (rising stock prices). Had these investors preferred the latter, they would have invested in common stocks instead of bonds.

If, as is frequently true, a portion of the settlement given debt holders takes the form of newly issued common stock in the reorganized company, then these investors are required to accept a type of security they usually avoid. Also, if the reorganized company were to fail again, debt holders may collect less than implied by the settlement since the value of these securities will fall.

Suppliers who had extended unsecured credit will normally collect a greater percentage of their debt than common stockholders but a smaller percentage than secured debt holders. Other parties harmed by bankruptcy include employees, pensioners, and local communities housing the company and its employees. Although these groups may suffer tremendous losses, the damage depends on the case's idiosyncrasies and the availability of alternatives.

The ability to identify potential bankrupts before they fail has great personal and social value. Most important, corporate managers might rectify problems and avert upcoming disasters. In addition, investors could better understand the riskiness of their stock or bond portfolios. Investors willing to assume greater risk could move into potential bankrupt situations, while more conservative investors could reallocate their portfolios into lower risk vehicles.

Bankruptcy detection became important in 1932 during the Great Depression when failure reached a level of 154 firms out of every 10,000. In modern times, the equivalent statistic is about 35 firms out of every 10,000. Although modern financial theorists have worked to unify this area of study, there are still three fundamental methods for predicting future failures: common sense, financial ratios, and statistical methods.[2]

Using Common Sense

Using a little common sense may well be the best predictor of bankruptcy. Those applying the commonsense method do not need sophisticated equipment and will not have to digest every financial report ever published by a company. Instead, the method requires being attuned to the realities of the marketplace for obvious signals of failure.

There are eight financial or company signs and five product signs to watch for with the commonsense technique. These are listed (in no particular order) in table 8–1. Remember, however, that even if all thirteen signs suggest bankruptcy, the company may survive and even prosper; that is, some of these items are only danger signs in particular contexts. This technique uses subjective measures. They will indicate a greater number of failures than actually occur. Still, common sense is of real use and value in evaluating the health of a company. And when it is

Table 8–1
Commonsense Bankruptcy Detectors

Financial or company signs

The company announces that it will be using a new accounting firm or has developed a new banking relationship.

A management dispute surfaces in a public forum.

Members of the board of directors suddenly resign.

The borrowing credit line is reduced.

Common stock is sold in a depressed market or for a price less than book value.

Company executives sell stock.

A major write-off of assets takes place.

The company is seen disregarding chapters 3–7 in this book.

Product signs

New competition enters the market.

Other firms seem to be selling products that are a generation ahead.

The research and development budget is proportionately less than the competitions.

Retailers always seem to be overstocked.

Friends and neighbors ask you to explain why you bought that company's product.

your company or one you have money invested in—or a competitor for that matter—every analytic technique is necessary.

Although some bankruptcies evolve suddenly, the majority seem to develop over a span of two or three years. Most have a multitude of causes, each of which contributes its share to the firm's ultimate demise. Some of the problems lead to new difficulties, which may contribute to the bankruptcy. For example, a firm with too little invested capital may resort to using excessive amounts of short-term debt. Both mistakes harm the firm, but neither completely or alone causes the failure.

The commonsense method avoids getting hung up on fine details. If, for example, a company is seen changing accounting firms, a blatant sign has been received. The prudent analyst knows to investigate further by examining the details. In some cases, this investigation discloses a dispute between the accountants and the company, the result of which is that the company's true financial health is worse than reported in the financial data (although there are other possibilities).

The commonsense signs for detecting bankruptcy should be treated like church bells or a dinner whistle. When you hear them, it is time to do something. Whether trouble is located or not, the commonsense sign has performed its function: it has forced you to be aware of what is really happening.

Finally, it should be obvious that for each of the thirteen signs listed in table 8–1, alternative, optimistic explanations exist. These alternate models are given in table 8–2. That is, the bells may be ringing or the whistles may be blowing for either positive or negative reasons. Still, when you hear them, it doesn't hurt to look.

Detecting Failures with Financial Ratios

Financial ratios are data or statistics derived from a firm's income statement, balance sheet, or sources and uses of funds table. Ratios are easy to produce and use. The information needed is found in financial statements made public in annual or quarterly reports, 10Q or 10K filings, or by computer time-sharing services that have data banks with this information.

Table 8–2
Optimistic Interpretations of Bankruptcy Signs

Sign	Explanation
New accountants	The company has grown and has decided to utilize a larger CPA firm.
Public dispute	The old guard is changing, and new blood is coming in.
Directors' resignation	A noncontributor has been forced off the board.
Lower credit line	Profits are large enough that the company's borrowing needs are reduced.
Selling common stock	A new investment of tremendous potential cannot wait for the market to rebound.
Asset write-off	Old mistakes have been recognized and dealt with.
Competition enters	The company is unable to meet the entire market demand. Once capacity catches up with demand, the competition can be dealt with.
Selling outdated products	The consumer is not yet ready for the technological revolution.
Lower R&D budget	Innovations are difficult to patent and require little time to implement once invented. Why bother?
Overstocked products	The company has a great distribution network.
Why this company?	Progress has not been perceived by all. Things are changing too rapidly for some.

The investigation of financial ratios should normally follow any commonsense bankruptcy signal that cannot be explained away. Moreover, financial managers and investment advisers constantly utilize financial ratios to keep tabs on the companies they follow.

Financial ratios are traditionally classified into six groups. The six groups measure different characteristics. Table 8–3 lists the groups and specifies their focus. There are more than several financial ratios in each category. Readers interested in reviewing them all should examine a good textbook on financial management or managerial finance.[3] Ratios able to detect bankruptcy comprise a subset of all ratios. These ratios are found in the liquidity, debt activity, and profitability categories. Tables 8–4 lists the best bankruptcy-detecting financial ratios.

Financial ratios can be used in two ways: to compare one firm to itself over time or to contrast several firms in the same year. The former approach identifies when a company's ratios change. Change may occur for any of three reasons: (1) the company's financial condition has weakened, (2) its financial condition has improved, or (3) in response to an external change, the company has made an internal response. To discover if a change is due to external events, interfirm comparisons are conducted. When, for example, every firm in an industry experiences a lower inventory turn (fewer dollars of sales for every dollar of inventory), instead of concluding that one company has lost control over its inventory, it may be better to assume that either the industry is experiencing a slowdown in sales or is about to introduce new products.

Table 8–5 indicates the financial ratio changes that suggest a firm's financial health is weakened. In most cases when such a change occurs, bankruptcy does not follow. The best analogy to explain why financial ratios predict more troubled companies than actually exist is to consider the job of the local weather forecaster. Sometimes, despite seemingly perfect conditions, a storm will suddenly strike an area. At other times, a projected blizzard fails to arrive because some unexpected event intervened. To do his job or her job, the weather forecaster must always predict

Table 8–3
Types of Financial Ratios

Type	Characteristic
Liquidity	Ability to meet current liabilities
Debt	How the firm is financed
Activity	How effectively assets are used
Profitability	Compares profits to sales, assets, and investment
Growth	Where the firm is going
Value	How the firm is judged by the market

Table 8–4
Bankruptcy-Detecting Financial Ratios

Liquidity Ratios	
Net working capital (sometimes called risk)	Current assets less current liabilities
Cash flow versus current liabilities	Net income plus depreciation and other noncash expenses divided by current liabilities
Debt Ratios	
Cash-flow coverage	Cash-flow divided by fixed charges, including interest and dividends
Times interest earned	Income before interest and taxes divided by interest charges
Short-term debt to assets	Current liabilities divided by total assets
Activity Ratios	
Inventory turn	Sales divided by inventory
Average collection period	Accounts receivable divided by average daily sales
Profitability Ratios	
Profit margin	Net income divided by sales

a storm whenever it seems likely. When the storm vanishes, the forecaster reacts in the same way as when an unexpected storm appears: apologize and go on with the job. The same holds for financial ratios: they predict some failures that are avoided and entirely miss other failures that occur.

The first four ratios in table 8–5 are concerned with the firm's ability to meet its creditors' expectations. Creditors expect a firm to pay its accounts payable, pay interest due, and redeem debt when it matures. If a firm is unable to fulfill these obligations, its creditors may attempt

Table 8–5
Changes in Financial Ratios Indicating Worsening Financial Condition

Ratio	*Change to Watch For*
Net working capital	Fewer dollars
Cash flow to current liabilities	Lower ratio
Cash-flow coverage	Lower ratio
Times interest earned	Lower ratio
Short-term debt to assets	Higher ratio
Inventory turn	Lower ratio
Average collection period	Higher ratio
Profit margin	Lower ratio

to seize its assets unless it seeks court protection. The biggest difference among the four ratios is that the first two include only current liabilities (debt due within a year), while the latter two include all debts. Since long-term creditors are easier to satisfy (they expect only interest payments), the first two ratios may be the most important bankruptcy indicator ratios.

Net working capital, the difference between a firm's current assets and current liabilities, measures the amount of money that would be left over if a firm liquidated its current assets at face value and used the proceeds to pay off its current liabilities. Although it is doubtful that current assets could be sold at face value in times of crisis, net working capital nonetheless constitutes a good indicator of financial health. The dollar value of net working capital also equals the amount of current assets financed with long-term debt. When a large proportion of current assets are financed with long-term debt (high net working capital), it is unlikely that a short-term liquidity crisis will ever arise.

The cash flow-to-current liabilities ratio is an alternative approach to gauging the ability of a firm to avoid a liquidity crisis. Current liabilities must be either renewed or refunded. Unless a firm is able to refund a liability, creditors will hesitate renewing it. This paradox is exactly the one many people have personally experienced with their credit cards. Banks usually respond to a request for a higher credit limit by a credit cardholder now at his or her limit by telling the cardholder to pay off the debt and then it will raise the limit. The bank is really telling the cardholder to prove that he or she is creditworthy by paying off the debt. The story is the same for companies: those able to repay their current liabilities may easily renew them. Companies in a liquidity bind are asked to repay instead of renew their obligations.

Cash flow is the money that the firm accumulates throughout the year after paying its bills. The typical calculation sets cash flow equal to net income plus depreciation and any other noncash expense. The higher the ratio of cash flow to current liabilities, the more likely that the firm is able to renew its current debt and pay off a portion of it.

The cash-flow coverage and times interest earned ratios are similar to the short-term ratios except they monitor total debt instead of current liabilities. The higher the ratio, the greater is the flow of money into the company relative to its obligations to pay interest, dividends, and refund debt. Thus, the higher the ratios, the less likely the firm is to become a bankruptcy risk.

The remaining debt ratio in the bankruptcy indicator list is the short-term debt to total assets ratio. Wickes's failure might have been avoided had this ratio not grown so unwisely. An increase in the proportion of total assets financed with short-term debt is rarely a good sign; however, failure is not necessarily imminent in such cases. There should be time either to raise additional equity funds or secure more long-term debt.

The final three ratios—the inventory turns, the average collection period, and the profit margin—like the short-term debt-to-total assets ratio, give warnings of worsening financial condition. They are not indicators of imminent collapse; however, if they persist, then collapse is more likely.

A lower inventory turn means that the firm (like Bowmar) is accumulating inventory relative to sales. Since profits are earned on sales and not on inventory, the company is making too heavy an investment in inventory. If the sign is missed and nothing is done, the situation may worsen and failure may result. By contrast, if management is alert, inventories can be reduced or sales may be promoted, and the ratio will improve.

A higher average collection period indicates that the firm's customers are taking longer to pay. Thus, the company is holding more receivables. Receivables are held as an investment. This investment encourages sales by customers needing credit, but lengthening the credit period rarely induces new sales, so it has few advantages for the firm. By contrast, there are sizable costs when the average collection period increases: interest on borrowed funds, more bad debts, and reduced liquidity. Thus, an increasing average collection period signals potential problems.

Finally, the profit margin is a good overall measure. It describes how well the firm is doing. A falling profit margin indicates that costs are rising relative to revenue. If the trend continues and the profit margin turns negative, cash will drain away. Ultimately the company fails unless the profit margin is positive. Positive cash flow can keep an unprofitable company alive only so long. Moreover, a firm with a persistent low profit margin is an economic failure even if it never actually goes bankrupt.

Statistical Methods

The scientific method is designed to uncover facts. When the scientific method is applied to bankruptcy, the objective is to find indicators that can always correctly identify an upcoming failure. There have been some notable successes: Altman's 1968 study, the Altman, Halderman, and Narayanan 1977 study, and the 1985 study by Coleen Pantalone and Marjorie Platt.[4]

The statistical method attempts to understand why a group of companies failed in the past and why another group of matched companies survived. Although a variety of statistical models have been employed, including multiple discriminating analysis, regression analysis, logit, and probit, each attempts to find a group of financial ratios that can always be reviewed to judge how likely a firm is to fail. Some of the methods produce a probability of failure; others produce a *Z score*, which indicates a greater chance of failure the lower the estimated Z score.

Several facts recur in most statistical studies. First, their predictive accuracy tends to fall off dramatically more than two years before a failure. The better studies—those able to exceed chance—seem to predict failure successfully only within two years of corporate failure. Three years before the crisis, the financial ratios of companies that will fail and those that will survive are not statistically different. To be useful, then, the models need to be rerun on a regular basis. Several private consulting firms specialize in this area.

Second, statistical models inevitably produce two types of errors. A Type I error means that a company predicted to fail does not. Type II error occurs when a company not predicted to fail goes bankrupt. There are private and social costs associated with each type of error. Better models have lower errors.

The Altman Study

Edward I. Altman is considered by many to be the father of modern bankruptcy analysis. Part of this credit is owed to his 1968 study, which provided a list of financial ratios that appeared to be able to discriminate between companies destined to survive and those expected to fail.[5] Table 8–6 lists these ratios in order of descending importance.

A company's Z score is calculated by multiplying the value of the five ratios for that company with Altman's estimated parameters. A high Z score can be interpreted as a low failure probability, and a low Z score means failure is likely.

In estimating parameters, Altman utilized a sample of sixty-six companies equally divided between failures and survivors. The failures spanned the interval 1946 through 1965. Not everyone agrees with Altman's results. Perhaps the two best reasons for questioning the usefulness of this model for a company today are that companies in the 1980s are different from those in the 1940s or 1950s and that the model is derived from only sixty-six cases.

The Altman, Haldeman, and Narayanan Study

This newer study employed a sample of fifty-three bankrupt firms and fifty-eight matched nonbankrupt companies.[6] The failures covered the

Table 8–6
Altman's Discriminating Ratios

$$\frac{\text{earning before interest and taxes}}{\text{total assets}}$$

$$\frac{\text{sales}}{\text{total assets}}$$

$$\frac{\text{market value of common stock}}{\text{total liabilities}}$$

$$\frac{\text{retained earnings}}{\text{total assets}}$$

$$\frac{\text{working capital}}{\text{total assets}}$$

period 1969 through 1975. Table 8–7 lists the important financial ratios in order of importance. Notice that some of the influences are positive, and others are negative; that is, some indicate failure while others indicate success.

Table 8–7
Altman, Haldeman, and Narayanan's Financial Indicators

$$\frac{\text{retained earnings}}{\text{total assets}}$$

$$\frac{\text{net income}}{\text{total assets}^{\text{a}}}$$

$$\frac{\text{equity}}{\text{total assets} - \text{current liability}}$$

$$\text{total assets}$$

$$\frac{\text{current assets}}{\text{current liabilities}}$$

$$\frac{\text{income before interest and taxes}}{\text{total interest payment}}$$

$$\frac{\text{net income}}{\text{total assets}}$$

[a]Calculated as a standard error.

A common inquiry concerns why the new study discovered a different set of financial ratios compared to the 1968 study. Only one ratio, retained earnings to total assets, overlaps the two studies; moreover, while this was the most important ratio in the 1977 study, it was practically the least important in 1968. A second more pragmatic question asks how long the new list of key ratios will be pertinent bankruptcy indicators.

Neither question is fully answerable because with statistical results, it is difficult to determine whether the findings are due to causation or merely correlation. This is especially true with a statistical methodology designed to select variables most able to discriminate between failure and success. While the introduced variables all come from financial reports, they are not developed from a theoretical foundation. They were chosen merely because they discriminate among a group of 111 firms. Thus, the results do not affirm a theory of bankruptcy but merely denote those variables statistically related to failure at this time. There are no alternatives to MDA or regression analysis, so it is necessary to use models like those of Altman and colleagues. Caution is advised, however, especially as the study ages.

The Pantalone and Platt Study

This 1985 study of saving and loan failures has two unique attributes.[7] First, it does not use a sample of failures. Instead the study relies on every savings and loans failure in the Federal Home Loan Bank Board, New England region in 1983 and 1985. Second, by examining failures within a single geographic region over a short time span, the study defuses many potential criticisms. The list of key failure indicators for savings and loans is provided in table 8–8.

During this period, approximately 20 percent of all savings and loans in the New England region failed. This awesome statistic suggests a need for greater regulator observation of savings and loans management and practices. Pantalone and Platt recommend that regulators calculate Z scores for savings and loans using the ratios in table 8–8. When low or falling Z scores are discovered, savings and loans examiners should become extremely cautious and begin to expect a failure.

Table 8–8
Pantalone and Platt's Key Savings and Loan Failure Indicators

Net worth/Total assets
Net interest income/Gross interest income
Borrowed money/Total savings
Real estate loans/Total assets

9
Strategies for the Near-Bankrupt

This chapter is directed to failing companies. Its purpose is to inform and educate. By examining how other companies in similar straits attempted to extricate themselves, failing companies may discover ways to preserve themselves. Also, managers of healthy companies can learn by observing how sick firms survive. Although some actions taken by failing companies are not directly transferable, even healthy firms may benefit in some cases from imitative actions. In addition to these potential advantages, there is one other reason for readers not associated with near-bankrupt firms to read this chapter: a business partner or associate may someday go bankrupt, and now is the time to learn how they can be expected to behave.

Near-bankrupt companies are not novices. Their health has been failing for at least several years. In addition to financial mistakes of the types described in chapters 3 through 7, many of these companies are also cursed with product or industry troubles. That is, near-bankrupts are often dinosaurs, companies destined to fail sooner or later. A nearly bankrupt company probably does not have any aces up its sleeve. The best it may have is a deuce or a tres.

Like a survivor from a sinking ship, the near-bankrupt company only has two options: sink or swim. Sinking means calling it quits and walking away from the problems. This is sometimes the better alternative. Dun & Bradstreet, in compiling its failure records, includes as failures all companies that cease operations without fully satisfying all creditors. This includes bankruptcies, liquidations, and walk-aways. In 1983, as many as 10 percent of all failures may have been walk-aways.

Companies opting to swim usually have a vision of better times that lie just ahead. The potential for disaster can be found here too. When the vision is merely chimerical, managers and employees may use it to transcend the feeling of hopelessness associated with death and dying. Some may even assume messianic personalities. They are driven by the hope that their own employment, pension fund, or seniority rights may not be terminated. For that reason, use extreme care when dealing with a near-bankrupt firm that thinks it sees salvation. Their day-to-day objective is very simple: survive until tomorrow. Sometimes they can hold on long enough to set straight their product or financial woes. In that case, they will become condors or tortoises, firms with remaining problems but not in immediate trouble.

More often than not, the near bankrupt survives because of a product recovery and not because of improved financial management. The reasons why financial miracles are unlikely are twofold. First, profits are earned by selling products. A firm lacking either a good product or healthy finances will still have sales difficulties even if financial woes are rectified. Second, lenders do not battle each other trying to be the first institution to lend money to a failing company. It might be possible for a near bankrupt to obtain some funds, at near usurious interest rates or by pledging all its assets, but it is doubtful that sufficient monies would be offered to a firm with a weak product or in an ailing industry to enable the firm to rise, phoenix-like, out of the ashes.

When lenders prefer to stay out of bankruptcy court, financial relief may be obtained to enable a dinosaur to revive. Largesse of this type is usually not provided by secured lenders who are protected by assets already pledged as loan collateral. Financial relief, if given, is usually provided by unsecured lenders who have the most to lose by pushing the near bankrupt into court. The legal and other costs of bankruptcy can be astronomical. When there are too many parties to a failure, it may not be possible to reach an agreement. Thus, even though it would be best, it may not be possible to keep the proceedings out of court.

Strategies That Might Help

All's fair in love and war and bankruptcy. Any strategy that keeps a failing firm alive is a good one, but the best strategies are those that provide longer-term relief. If the managers must fight for survival each day, they will not have the time or energy to discover product improvements capable of permanently changing the firm's outlook. It is therefore in the best interest of the firm to seek remedies having lasting impact.

There are three varieties of solutions. The first type involves the company's assets, the valuables owned by the company. Second are solutions using the company's liabilities, its debt to others. Third, are solutions to be found within the company itself. Each of these choices is discussed in turn by using a new device, minicases. A minicase presents major ideas with little advance introduction. The objectives of the minicase are to present a strategy and to describe its use by way of an example from a real business. Readers interested in following a particular strategy should further examine its ramifications.

Asset Maneuvers

A company's assets are those items it owns that have value. Assets may be physical items (such as factories, inventory, or equipment), accounting records (such as accounts receivable), or intangibles such as goodwill, patents, or technologies. Since assets have value, they may be sold, traded, loaned, or used to secure borrowed funds.

Asset maneuvers are probably the best remedies since they involve structuring deals that at least on paper appear to benefit both parties: the white knight and the near bankrupt. On the negative side, asset-based solutions are usually one-shot deals. Once a company has sold or otherwise disposed of its best assets, it has little else of value to sell. Also, little may be left of a company after selling off prime divisions. Still, there may not be any alternative to engaging in an asset maneuver.

Table 9–1 lists, in order of increasing severity, three fairly commonplace asset-based maneuvers. The first technique, collateralizing a new loan with assets, is not severe at all. In fact, it is not imposed on failing companies alone. Therefore it is a painless remedy unless it is signaling further troubles. Selling off assets is a more radical treatment since it leaves behind less of value. Liquidation is the ultimate asset-based remedy. Interestingly, some successful companies have chosen to liquidate their assets. A successful company might liquidate itself if it believed that the stock market would never value it as high as would acquiring companies. Second, liquidation in some cases allows profits to be distributed to shareholders before paying federal taxes. If creditors receive less from a liquidation than owed, then it is reasonable to suspect that the liquidation was a solution adopted by a failing company.

Storage Technology

Storage Technology filed a Chapter 11 petition in November 1984, another victim of competition with IBM. A worldwide company with thousands of employees, Storage Technology had prospered offering computer disk drives that were compatible with IBM mainframe computer systems.

Table 9–1
Using Assets in a Crisis

1. Collateralize a new loan using assets.
2. Sell off an unsuccessful division. Later, if necessary, sell a successful division.
3. Completely liquidate the company's assets.

Numerous difficulties beset the company in the 1980s. Probably the most severe of these problems were generated by both the company's failed attempt to enter the mainframe computer market and IBM's introduction of new disk storage devices that outperformed Storage Technology's equipment.

In November 1984, Storage Technology filed for court protection. Soon thereafter, the company apparently made an attempt to obtain additional financing by using all its remaining unsecured assets as collateral for a $150 million working capital loan. These funds would enable Storage Technology to continue marketing, producing, and developing its products, almost as if it had never filed the Chapter 11 petition, while a reorganization plan is worked out between the creditors and the company. If additional funds cannot be found, the company will need to lay off a sizable portion of its work force to conserve working capital.

Pan American Airways

Pan American Airways has been dying for almost a decade. Although one of the world's first airlines, Pan Am lacked the domestic routes to feed passengers into its international flights. Moreover, in the 1960s Pan Am became heavily indebted when an overly ambitious expansion left the firm with an underutilized fleet of expensive aircraft. Also, a merger with National Airlines failed to yield hoped-for benefits.

Pan Am had earlier exhausted its debt capacity by borrowing to acquire aircraft. Moreover, with the 71 million shares of common stock selling for as little as $1.75, additional equity sales were not realistic. Thus, when a series of financial crises ensued over the past decade, Pan Am's financial position was eroded as management sold off one valuable asset after another. Among the assets sold were the Intercontinental Hotel chain, the Pan Am building in New York City, and many used aircraft. Pan Am has virtually no expendable assets left to sell. It will have to be profitable in the future or else suffer the consequences.

Crompton

Crompton began its textile business in 1807. In late 1984, the firm filed a Chapter 11 petition and reported that it would attempt to liquidate its assets. The Crompton story mirrors the transition of the United States out of the smokestack era and into the high-technology era. Foreign competition and export difficulties caused by the strong U.S. dollar made it difficult for the firm to do business. For the four years preceding the Chapter 11 filing, Crompton lost money: about $885,000 in 1981, $12 million in 1982, $7.8 million in 1983, and $15.7 million in 1984.

Management concluded that it would not be possible to continue in business. Thus, as the Chapter 11 petition was filed, the company announced that it had suspended all operations. It must have been impossible to stem the cash outflow. An agreement was reached with creditors to liquidate all assets within six months. Management stated that it hoped creditors could be paid in full and that there would be something left over for common stockholders. While Crompton reported positive net worth (assets in excess of liabilities), creditors might not receive all they are due. After all, assets unable to produce a profit may not have much value in the marketplace.

Liability Maneuvers

Liabilities include all the sources of finance or funding that a firm has used. In principle, there are three types of liabilities: current liabilities, debt, and equity. *Current liabilities* include all funds that the company has obtained that must be repaid within a one-year period. This category includes accounts payable (funds owed to suppliers), notes payable (money obtained from the bank), and accrued expenses. Many times a firm's suppliers and employees know the company is in trouble even before the firm itself knows. Thus, while the company may be able to obtain some additional financing from current liabilities, in most cases, the palliative will be short-lived at best.

Debt is money borrowed for periods longer than one year. Table 6–2 lists three types of debt. In fact, the number of types of debt available is virtually unlimited. It is always possible for a company to structure its debt in such a way as to take advantage of its own circumstances and the needs of investors. For example, some silver companies have offered debt that at maturity is redeemed for silver bullion instead of money; some debt is convertible into common stock, and some debt is never redeemed but pays interest forever. Debt is a good source of finance for troubled companies because the debt can be constructed to provide investors with a sufficient return to encourage them to lend to a near-bankrupt company. One possible strategy is to issue income bonds. These bonds pay interest only when the firm earns an income. Should income not be earned, the interest need not be paid, and the debtors cannot force the firm into bankruptcy. To compensate investors for the extra risk, income bonds pay higher interest rates than normal bonds. Similarly, convertible bonds may attract investors to troubled companies. Should the company be revived, the investors can convert their relatively well-protected bonds into high-priced common stock at a very advantageous exchange rate.

Equity is money obtained from owners. Equity funds are obtained by selling shares of stock in a company. A good way to measure how desperate a firm is for equity funds is to compare the selling price of the stock to the per share book value of the company (called the *market-to-book-value ratio*). A market-to-book-value ratio less than 1 means that new shares were sold for less than old shares were worth on the books. Firms that sell stock in desperation often receive less than book value for the new shares. Selling stock in a near bankrupt may well be the worst approach from the company's point of view since common stock is the lowest-priority claim in the event of bankruptcy. Thus, it may be nearly impossible to sell stock in a near bankrupt unless the owners are willing to give away virtually their entire company for a new infusion of equity capital. Should the owners prefer not to sell equity, however, assuming a buyer could be found, and should the firm fail as a result, the eventual reorganization plan that emerges from negotiations between creditors may well take away the company from the old owners anyway.

Liability maneuvers are more extreme than asset maneuvers since they involve either bringing in new owners or confronting debtors; however, a liability maneuver may remedy the current problem and give the firm an opportunity to succeed in the marketplace. Table 9–2 lists five liability-based strategies that may help failing firms obtain financial relief.

Mattel

Mattel, long famous for its toys, successfully entered the home video game market in the late 1970s; however, lagging consumer interest and intense competition among suppliers caused an industry shake-out in the early 1980s. Mattel was one of the big losers. For fiscal year 1984 (ending

Table 9–2
Using Equity or Liabilities in a Crisis

1. Sell new shares of common stock.
2. Obtain a loan guarantee from the government or an interested third party.
3. Negotiate an extension plan with lenders.
4. Negotiate a composition plan with lenders.
5. File a Chapter 11 bankruptcy petition.

Note: For purposes of this table, it is assumed that the firm has already sold as much debt as is possible. Thus, the only category of debt listed is a government-backed loan. A government loan guarantee is a way to get investors to accept even more debt in one company than they really want.

February 1984), Mattel lost $403.5 million as a result of writing off numerous assets. Since this loss was greater than Mattel's total net worth (accumulated profits and owners' equity), Mattel reported a negative net worth of $136 million.

A negative net worth implies two important facts. First, the company must have assets that are more valuable than is registered on the balance sheet; otherwise it would formally be bankrupt. Second, having negative net worth signifies a troubled firm that is near bankrupt. Mattel reacted as might be expected. The home video division was shut down, stemming further losses. Then the firm sold off all its assets other than the toy division. But still more money was needed. Mattel chose to sell equity. In exchange for $231 million, it gave a group of investors 45 percent of the company. Although these investors might ultimately take total control of the firm, the plan raised enough new equity to make net worth positive, alleviate a working capital problem, and pay off a term loan that was coming due.

With this cash infusion, Mattel should survive. If in the future it again becomes prosperous, both the old and new owners will benefit. Both should be pleased. After all, 55 percent of something is worth far more than 100 percent of nothing.

Chrysler

Most people are aware of Chrysler's brush with death, but a brief recounting of the story might be of use to some readers. After the 1973 oil embargo, gasoline prices rose dramatically. Reacting to the new prices at the pump, consumer preferences switched to smaller, more efficient vehicles. Over the next four or five years, fuel prices remained steady but fell relative to inflation. Slowly consumers returned to their old habits of buying larger vehicles. Chrysler saw this change and gambled that it would continue by building larger cars. There may have been some wishful thinking in this decision since making larger cars is more profitable than building smaller vehicles.

When the Shah of Iran was deposed in 1979, oil prices doubled, and Chrysler's troubles began again. Chrysler was caught flat, unable to deliver the smaller vehicles that had once again become popular. While it had plans for a new generation of smaller cars, the K series, it lacked the capital to begin development. Moreover, it was not generating profits from its slow-selling existing car lines.

Chrysler seemed to be finished. Bankers were unwilling to extend further credit, and a large enough equity offering, given Chrysler's low stock price, was hardly practical. Management essentially had two choices: obtain a loan backed by a government loan guarantee or file a

Chapter 11 bankruptcy petition. Proponents of the loan guarantee program believed that massive unemployment would result from a Chrysler failure and that the government would actually save money by supporting Chrysler. Whether or not this was true, the U.S. government did earn a large profit when warrants to Chrysler stock it had been given were sold.

Sonoma Vineyards

In 1984, Sonoma Vineyards was unable to repay the principal on its debt. To let creditors know the extent of their concern, management announced it was contemplating filing a Chapter 11 bankruptcy petition. Negotiations between creditors and the company followed, producing an extension plan coupled with the sale of assets. *Extension* means delaying either interest or principal payments for a period of time. Eventually payments resume, but lost interest may or may not ever be repaid.

Sonoma announced that it would dispose of all assets—a retail tool store chain and a mail order business—other than its wine business. Lenders would allow Sonoma to extend repayment until December 31, 1984. The advantages to the plan were these:

1. Bankruptcy costs could be saved.
2. Assets could be disposed of in an orderly manner capable of maximizing selling price.
3. Wine business suppliers and customers would maintain their perceptions of Sonoma, thereby not jeopardizing future wine sales.

Extensions are often good for both lenders and borrowers. Given a breather in which to set things right, many near bankrupts without fundamental problems can recover; however, dinosaurs can never be saved. The dilemma for the lender is to discern the dinosaur from the firm that merely made a mistake. Probably the best way to make this choice is through frank discussions with the firm's managers about the company's business plan. Statistical models might also provide some assistance.

Astro Drilling

Declining oil prices in the early 1980s caused severe financial strain for numerous oil and gas exploration, development, and production companies. Many of these firms, including MGF Oil, Seneca Oil, and Patrick Petroleum, failed. Some resorted to bankruptcy filings, while others, as in the case of Patrick Petroleum, chose to liquidate their assets.

Astro Drilling, an oil rig operator, used a composition plan to attempt a turnaround. *Composition* converts old debt into new lower interest debt, equity, or both. Arthur Young & Company, Astro's auditors, had issued a qualified opinion about the 1983 annual report saying that Astro's ability to meet its financial obligation depended on an improved oil market. Astro had lost over $5 million in 1983, partly because utilization of its oil rigs was too low and partly because it was saddled with too much debt. Improvement in the oil market was well beyond Astro's control, but it could seek a remedy to its overutilization of debt.

Astro has $4.25 million in subordinated debt, $17 million in bank debt, and approximately 2.75 million shares of common stock. What it needed was less debt and more stock; however, its stock was selling for less than $1 per share, so selling new shares to redeem the old debt would have been impractical. Instead following Astro's negotiations with lenders, the subordinated debt was converted into 2.125 million shares of stock, and the bank debt became 3 million shares of stock and a new $16 million loan that was backed by all the company's assets.

In the long run, all parties seem to have benefited from this strategy. Without a composition plan, Astro would have probably been forced to file a Chapter 11 petition to seek protection from its debtors. Thus the plan helped Astro since it could remain in business and hope for an upturn in its fortunes.

If Astro had failed, the subordinated debtors would probably have recovered little of their investment. *Subordinated debt* means that its holders must wait for senior debt, in this case the bank debt, to be repaid fully before participating in a distribution of assets. Clearly these debtors were better off with the plan than with a failure.

Finally, the bankers might have forced Astro into bankruptcy, but they would gain little by that action. The details of the plan require the banks to forgo just $1 million, and it is conceivable that they will own 38 percent of a successful company. Their own risk is that a continued cash drain will further reduce Astro's liquidation value in the event it ultimately fails.

Holywell

Real estate development is a tricky business. Some people succeed at it, gaining fabulous wealth, while others fail. The margin of difference between the two groups may be quite close. Ironically a strategy of filing a Chapter 11 bankruptcy petition may be one way for more real estate developers to succeed.

Holywell and Theodore Gould, its principal owner, ran into trouble building the Miami Center, a hotel and office complex in Florida. When the bankers who had extended a $197 million construction loan moved to foreclose the project, Holywell and Gould filed Chapter 11 petitions. This action gave them time to seek additional financing since a company is protected from its creditors while working out a plan of reorganization.

A few months later, Gould announced a $250 million offer for the project from a large concern. Apparently several other larger offers may follow. Using these funds as a base, Gould reported that he intends to file a reorganization plan for removing his company from bankruptcy within the next several months. The courts thus provided him with the time needed to attend to his business in an orderly manner. Presumably he will walk away from the project a success.

Company Maneuvers

Sometimes nonfinancial strategies are needed in order to get near-bankrupt companies back on their feet. Company maneuvers can affect any facet of a struggling firm's existence, from its work force to its executive office. Often these ideas must come from the board of directors or from paid outside consultants. The board of directors may not be too helpful in a crisis, however, for two reasons. First, members of the board were probably not chosen because of their expertise in crisis management. Thus they lack the skills or experience necessary to develop an innovative plan quickly. Second, the board is probably composed of persons who have personal stakes in the success of the current plan. Thus they will have trouble thinking of new ideas essential for success.

Good consultants are hard to find. Many consultants are right out of business school and lack practical experience in problem solving. Moreover, few business schools offer special courses to prepare students for bankruptcy management. Should a good consultant be found, however, he or she may offer insights that will never occur to management or members of the board.

Table 9–3 lists five company maneuvers that may apply in some cases. Company maneuvers are probably more dependent on a particular firm's idiosyncrasies than either asset or liability maneuvers. For that reason, in reading the minicases in this section, recognize the special circumstances applying to each case. If none of the suggestions in table 9–3 is appropriate in a given situation, the situation may not be hopeless. Other company-specific maneuvers exist, waiting to be discovered.

Eagle Computer

Eagle Computer was well on its way to becoming the primary competitor to IBM in the IBM-compatible personal computer business when it

Table 9–3
Refocusing the Company in Times of Crisis

1. Develop a new company strategy.
2. Remove the management team that shepherded the firm into trouble.
3. Pressure the labor force and suppliers for concessions. If they seem recalcitrant, threaten to shut down or to move to the Orient.
4. Shut down.
5. Merge with another company.

Note: The table might also have included reducing operations as a maneuver to try in times of crisis. Its omission was purposeful since the table describes actions that companies should try after they have halted all unprofitable and nonessential endeavors.

suffered a disastrous courtroom defeat in a copyright infringement suit. Nevertheless, it persevered and attempted to continue to do battle with IBM. The plan did not work. Eagle's losses were tremendous. A continuation of business as usual was impossible.

Rather than close the company, management decided to concentrate on specialty markets for its computer products. In other words, the firm chose to not do further battle with IBM but to seek out market niches that IBM had missed. It adopted a new strategy whose major objective is not profits but survival. Without altering its strategy, Eagle would have folded. Even with the new more limited approach, it might still fail.

Farah Manufacturing

In most bankruptcies presented in this book, existing management is removed and new managers are hired just before or as soon as the firm files for court protection. Thus there would be little learned by presenting a similar case to depict how a struggling company might benefit by removing bad managers. It might be informative, however, to consider what happens when a firm removes a good manager.

Farah Manufacturing had been a troubled company. In addition to losing money throughout much of the 1970s, the company was the center of a bitter union-management dispute. A new president, Ray Williams, was hired in 1978. As a result of his keen management talents, the firm prospered. In 1983 the firm reported record sales and had experienced steadily rising income throughout most of Williams's tenure.

The only trouble was that Williams was not a member of the family that controlled Farah. Thus, when he resigned "to pursue personal business opportunities," there was consternation on Wall Street.[1] Farah's stock plummeted 24 percent in just one day, closing at $20.75 after falling $6.50.

Good management is the key to success. With it, profits can be earned. Without it, even the highest-flying eagle might be transformed into another creature.

Frontier Airlines

Frontier Airlines had never been too profitable, but deregulation seemed to hit it harder than most other airlines. Despite winning major concessions (20 percent reductions in wages and benefits) from its employees after deregulation was implemented, the airline lost over $13 million in 1983 and continued to lose money in 1984. Since labor tends to average about 25 percent of total cost in the airline business, 20 percent wage and benefit cutbacks lower average cost by about 5 percent.

Frontier also tried new product strategies, introducing a separate nonunion carrier and locating flights out of new cities, but none of these moves seemed capable of making the carrier profitable. A continuation of the cash drain could not be permitted, but the only source of additional relief seemed to be the work force again. Management apparently feared the response of labor to a second request for lower wages and benefits and thus announced that it was considering liquidating the line unless further concessions could be obtained.

A second round of wage cuts might return Frontier to profitability, but this request seems equally likely to produce permanent friction between labor and management and leads one to wonder how costs might possibly have gotten so out of control that a 40 percent reduction in labor costs is required for survival.

Wien Airlines

The Wien Airlines example is practically the same as the Frontier example, just as recommendation 4 in table 9–3 is an extreme version of recommendation 3. Wien had been losing money rapidly. To attempt to halt the process, it had enacted a series of bankruptcy management steps:

1. It sold half of its aircraft.
2. It reduced by 60 percent the number of cities it served.
3. It discontinued certain unprofitable operations.
4. It sold several assets.
5. It requested relief from its labor unions.

Despite these steps, the losses continued. On November 6, 1984, the firm announced that it would halt all operations for twenty-five days to stem the losses. What the next step will be is anyone's guess. The firm might be liquidated, sold, or sent into a Chapter 11 bankruptcy.

Data Terminal Systems

Data Terminal Systems (DTS) was a pioneer in the check-out scanner business. While DTS was profitable in its early years, it soon encountered competition from major technology companies, such as IBM, National Cash Register, and Burroughs. Profits turned to losses, and the firm's customers and suppliers began to question its survivability.

Progress was hard to make until a white knight in the form of National Semiconductor purchased DTS. National Semiconductor paid a relatively low price for DTS, indicating that there were few other bidders.

One reason why many near bankrupts merge before failing is that their historic losses are tax-deductible expenses for the acquiring company, provided that the two firms are in the same business. A corporation in the 46 percent tax bracket might be able to finance nearly an entire acquisition using the tax advantage of writing off the acquired company's previous losses. Recent proposals to lower or do away with the corporate income tax would, if enacted, reduce the number of near bankrupts acquired for tax reasons.

Synopsis

It is never too late to try to save a company. The endless variety of asset, liability, and company maneuvers that exist provides opportunities for the entrepreneur's creativity and endurance. The ideas given in the tables in this chapter are but a small share of the total number of ways to keep an unhealthy firm alive.

A sick company must uncover its fundamental shortcomings. When financial difficulties are at the root of the problem, the company is a condor; when product troubles exist, the company is a tortoise. Although different skills are required to solve financial or product problems, key managers must address these issues if the solutions are to be anything more than short-term palliatives.

Both the condor and the tortoise should seek out and use the advice of outsiders, despite the fact that good advice might be expensive. The reason is simple: an outsider may be able to see a problem that is hidden or is at least not obvious to an internal. The insider might discover the problem in the future, but a troubled firm may not have a long future.

10
Investing in Bankrupt Companies

Every three or four months, the popular financial press circulates what it touts as a new idea: there's money to be made investing in bankrupt companies. This chapter examines this advice. The notion is actually quite appealing. Securities of most bankrupt companies trade at bargain prices. Some bankrupt stocks sell for 6 cents per share, and bankrupt company bonds may sell for a fraction of their original value. One good friend, who has prospered buying securities of this type, always remarks, "It's easier for a 6 cent stock to double in value than it is for a $50 stock." His belief may be true, but it is important to be aware that most firms filing a Chapter 11 bankruptcy petition either are eventually liquidated or are reorganized without any compensation or securities given to original stockholders. In these cases, investors in the prereorganization company's equity lose everything.

In my graduate business school managerial finance class, when asked about the strategy of investing in this or that bankrupt company, my usual response is, "Why not? What can go wrong? They're already bankrupt." These comments summarize the basic rationale for bankruptcy investing. In part, the ideas are true; however, not all bankrupts are equal. Some may confront further troubles ahead, while others may be safely on the road to recovery.

The ultimate test of bankruptcy investing is to compare the average returns earned by investors in bankrupt companies to the average return that might have been earned investing in nonbankrupt companies. Using a sample of eleven bankruptcies, tables 10–1 and 10–2 calculate the average annual return (compound annual percentage increase or decrease in investment value) on both stocks and bonds.

Three Rules for Bankruptcy Investing

Although a sample of eleven bankruptcies is not sufficient to draw definitive conclusions, it is hard to ignore the stark differences between

Table 10–1
Returns from Bankrupt Stocks

Company (Failure Rate)	Price per Share Prior to Failure	Price in January 1982	Average Return
Penn Central Transportation (June 1970)	$ 1.50	$ 1.32	– 1%
King Resources (September 1971)	1.81	0.31	– 19
Miller-Wohl (September 1972)	6.75	185.34	42
Equity Funding (April 1973)	25.38	3.77	– 24
Unishops (November 1973)	1.63	1.75	1
Interstate Stores (Toys-R-Us) (May 1974)	1.63	22.34	39
Daylin (February 1975)	1.50	4.06	16
Bowmar Instruments (February 1975)	4.38	2.47	– 9
W.T. Grant (October 1975)	3.38	0.00	– 100
United Merchants & Manufacturing (July 1977)	5.38	4.13	– 5
Neisner Brothers (December 1977)	3.25	6.64	20

Source: Derived from Table 9–1, page 244, in Edward A. Altman, *Corporate Financial Distress: A Complete Guide to Predicting, Avoiding, and Dealing with Bankruptcy*, John Wiley & Sons Publishers, New York, 1983. Used with permission. Average return from Ibbotson and Sinquefield, 1982.

Note: average return of stock sample = – 3.64 percent per year; average return entire stock market = 10.9 percent per year.

the returns earned investing in the stocks and bonds of bankrupt companies. The most salient comparisons are summarized below:

The average return on bankrupt stocks is negative.

The average return on bankrupt bonds is positive.

The average bankrupt stock underperformed (earned less than) the average stock.

The average bankrupt bond earned more than the average bond.

This sample of eleven companies includes mostly reorganized firms. Since bond investors invariably receive a greater percentage payout than

Table 10–2
Returns from Bankrupt Bonds

Company (Failure Rate)	Price per Share Prior to Failure	Price in January 1982	Average Return
Penn Central Transportation (June 1970)	$ 720.00	$3,585.00	15%
King Resources (September 1971)	90.00	1,585.00	32
Miller-Wohl (September 1972)[a]			
Equity Funding (April 1973)	1,098.00	935.00	−2
	800.00	335.00	−10
Unishops (November 1973)[a]			
Interstate Stores (Toys-R-Us) (May 1974)	220.00	3,919.00	45
	450.00	3,350.00	28
Daylin (February 1975)	700.00	1,056.00	6
	220.00	1,164.00	26
Bowmar Instruments (February 1975)[a]			
W.T. Grant (October 1975)	360.00	1,000.00	18
	317.50	140.00	−12
	235.00	140.00	−7
United Merchants & Manufacturing (July 1977)	890.00	636.00	−8
	502.50	280.00	−15
Neisner Brothers (December 1977)[a]			

Source: Derived from Table 9–1, page 244, in Edward A. Altman, *Corporate Financial Distress: A Complete Guide to Predicting, Avoiding, and Dealing with Bankruptcy*, John Wiley & Sons Publishers, New York, 1983. Used with permission. Average return from Ibbotson and Sinquefield, 1982.

Note: average return of bond sample = 8.9 percent per year (includes interim dividends or interest payments); average return of entire bond market = 2.6 percent per year.

[a]No public debt.

stock investors in the event of a liquidation, a comparison of all bankrupt companies (those both liquidated and reorganized) would show an even greater advantage to bankrupt bonds over bankrupt stocks than did the more limited comparison in tables 10–1 and 10–2. Thus, the first rule for potential bankruptcy investors is: *Buy bonds, not stocks.*

Knowledgeable investors might concede that bankruptcy bonds are better investments on average than bankruptcy stocks; however, some investors may nonetheless argue that if a superior bankrupt can be found, one that will develop into an eagle, then a greater return can be earned on that company's stock than on its bonds. This might be true, but in tables 10–1 and 10–2, the greatest annual return is earned on a bond, the first bond, labeled case a, for the company now called Toys-R-Us Inc., a bankrupt that became an eagle. Thus, rule 2 can be articulated as follows: *Bankrupt bonds and stocks have similar potentials for substantial returns.*

Neither bankrupt bonds nor stocks always provide the investor with positive returns. In fact, only five of eleven bankrupt stocks and seven of thirteen bankrupt bonds in the tables earned positive returns. In both cases, the ratio of success (a positive return) to failure is approximately 50 percent. Thus rule 3 can be stated: *Bankruptcy investments earn profits about half the time.*

Using Portfolios

Modern financial theory has demonstrated that the investor can minimize risk for a given level of return by constructing a stock portfolio. To develop a portfolio, the investor merely distributes his or her total investment across a number of different companies. Thus, if a reader decides to embark on a strategy of investing in bankrupt companies (hopefully bonds), he or she should spread the investment dollars around a number of companies.

The principal behind stock portfolios is not new. "Don't put all your eggs in one basket" has an identical meaning. If your investment funds are concentrated on one company, you could be wiped out if that firm does not succeed. By contrast, with a portfolio, it is unlikely that the entire investment will ever be completely wiped out; however, a lower average return is earned with a portfolio since a set of winners is mixed with a set of losers.

Choosing Which Bankrupts to Buy

Several characteristics distinguish good potential bankruptcy investments from companies that should be avoided (see table 10–3). Each characteristic contributes to the firm's ability to survive, solve problems, and eventually succeed.

Asset Value

The most important consideration in determining whether a company in bankruptcy court will ever emerge whole and healthy is its real net

Table 10–3
Characteristics of Good Bankrupt Companies

The real value of the company's assets exceeds the value of its liabilities.

People at the helm demonstrate keen perception, astute abilities, and a willingness to work with others.

New sources of working capital are found.

Operating income is earned while the company is still in Chapter 11 proceedings.

Sales growth is positive, possibly after a once-and-for-all decrease caused by an asset sale.

Unit costs begin to decrease.

General overhead expense decreases.

worth. *Real net worth* equals the difference between the company's real asset value and its total liabilities. If the company has positive real net worth, a reorganization plan can probably be instituted. In this event, creditors are less likely to push for a liquidation.

It may even be possible to save some companies with a negative net worth. Equally important are the future cash flows (net profits plus depreciation) that the company might be able to earn. Cash flows are the funds that will be retained by the firm as it carries out its business. Cash flows can be used to reinvest in the firm's future or to pay cash dividends to owners. Without positive future cash flows, even companies with tremendous real net worth are not candidates for saving. Conversely, a company without any real net worth but with high future cash flows is a prime candidate for revival.

Asset valuation is tricky. First, you must know what assets a company owns. Then you must determine what each asset is worth. Investors and other outsiders have difficulty trying to estimate the true value of a company's assets. For that matter, insiders do not always have an easy time estimating the value of assets, but at least they know what a company owns. The problem for outsiders is that it is not always possible to uncover what assets companies own by reading public reports. Often the most that can be learned is that a company has so many dollars invested in fixed plant and equipment. But the key ingredients to value determination—what type of plant and equipment, how old it is, and where it is located—are not described.

Probably the best advice is to be skeptical. Don't expect gems to be uncovered once the sheets are thrown off. A troubled firm may already have disposed of its best assets in its search for new financing. Moreover, if the firm has valuable assets, it has little to gain by hiding them at this point since creditors, like investors, are searching for reasons not to force the firm into liquidation.

Good Management

Having good people running the firm is essential. Even a 747 aircraft, a near-perfect technological wonder, cannot fly itself; a good pilot must be at the helm. Among the traits corporate leaders must possess when they are managing a bankrupt firm are an ability to see beyond the obvious, possession of a multitude of business skills (including finance, marketing, and production), and an ability to work, motivate, and negotiate with others.

A myopic chief executive might be able to run a successful business; however, a bankrupt company run by such a person will probably not survive long. If afflicted with shortsightedness, the executive will not be able to perceive any benefits from reorganizing the company and thus can be expected to follow the easy route of liquidation.

And indeed, liquidation is easy, because once a decision has been reached, it requires no further thought. By contrast, in order to convince the many creditor committees of the reorganization worthiness of a company, the executive must develop a business plan that takes advantage of the company's abilities in ways that have not yet been exploited. Not only must fresh ideas be discovered, but the executive must work to organize and plan their implementation.

The chief executive must thus possess a number of business skills. He or she may now be forced to perform tasks that a staff person would be available to do in a healthy company. Now these responsibilities will now rest on the executive's shoulders. The executive knows that the firm will not be given too many more chances. Thus, it will be in his or her best interest, as well as in the best interest of the company, for all plans to be approved by the executive. A general knowledge of all facets of business will be required to facilitate executive review.

Finally, the need for the executive to be able to work with, motivate, and negotiate with others arises because the executive must succeed both internally and externally. Internal success requires an ability to define problems and uncover solutions. These tasks must not only be performed with other people but cannot succeed unless the whole team is pulling together. The external battle with creditors requires consummate negotiating skills since creditors may be disinterested in the company's future. The executive must show creditors that it is in their best financial interest to permit the firm to be reorganized. Neither task is easy; both require cross-task coordination.

Outsiders are as ill equipped to judge the quality of a company's executive as they are to evaluate the firm's assets. Although far from a perfect rule, it might be wise to mistrust the abilities of executives who managed companies into bankruptcy. Investors should look for bankrupt companies who have brought in new managers, particularly if those new managers have a track record in the same business field. Moreover, the best companies may be those who bring in bankruptcy specialists, people with experience in reviving failing companies. These persons may be thought of analogously to relief pitchers in baseball, persons trained to handle special events.

New Working Capital

Working capital, the difference between a company's current assets and its current liabilities, is the lifeblood of a corporation. Without it, the firm cannot survive. Sometimes firms with healthy products, growing sales, and good management stumble as a result of the onset of a working capital crisis. In other situations, a working capital problem is only one of many symptoms of the fact that a company is a dinosaur. Regardless of type of firm, unless the working capital problem is resolved, the company cannot return to normal.

Troubled firms obtain working capital from lenders. Lending to a bankrupt firm is something like buying a ticket on the *Titanic*: you know your chances for survival are slim. Thus, new working capital loans to failing companies are usually secured (collateralized) by assets; however, since older creditors have a stake and a voice in the company's future, management cannot always bail out of a crisis by mortgaging assets to new lenders. Thus, how many dollars will be lent and what assets will secure the loan are the subjects of negotiation. Since a failure to reach an agreement usually means the end of a firm's existence, outsiders can use the announcement of a new lending arrangement as a sign that the company has a long-term future.

Improved Operating Characteristics

If a firm is to survive in the long term, it must have a product to sell that consumers want, and it must be able to make a profit selling this product. Profits equal the difference between revenue and cost. Thus, to survive in the long term, a troubled company must improve its *operating characteristics*: its sales, costs, and profit.

One of the first actions most firms take once they have filed for bankruptcy court protection is to write off worthless assets. The idea behind this strategy is that no further harm can come from reporting all previous mistakes. Companies will shed whole divisions, single stores, or just obsolete inventory at the time of a bankruptcy filing. Thus, it is not too surprising to discover that the sales of a company recently filed under Chapter 11 are lower than they were in a comparable period a year ago. Once a short grace period passes, however, the firm needs to begin to show growth in sales. If it cannot find new markets or develop new products, it will be hard pressed to resurrect itself.

The growth need not be spectacular, just consistent. Stability is preferred to speed in this situation. Success allows companies to get lazy. Complacency leads to excessive costs and unnecessary expenses. For example, how many companies really need a fleet of corporate jets, executives who belong to country clubs, or costly art objects scattered about corporate headquarters? Bodies contain fat as a source of substance in lean periods. Corporations must treat their fat in the same manner. When troubles arise, firms must immediately start to reduce wasteful expenditures and become leaner and tougher.

The results of this transformation should be obvious to outsiders. Not only should cost and general overhead expenses decline compared to the old days, but cost as a percentage of sales should also fall. Therefore, the company should be able to turn out its product at a lower cost per unit. Unless it can make this transition, it may not be able to survive.

Since profits equal the difference between revenues and costs, higher revenues and lower costs should result in greater profits. Therefore operating profits should improve.

Companies under the protection of the bankruptcy courts do not pay interest on their outstanding debt, although unpaid interest becomes a liability of the firm to be resolved in the course of a reorganization. It is not too surprising, therefore, to find bankrupt firms reporting quarterly or annual profits. To avoid overestimating potential future profits, careful investors will reduce reported profits by a reasonable estimate of what interest expenses will be after a reorganization plan has been improved.

11
Conclusion

After presenting a lecture, every instructor wonders if the lesson has been absorbed. When one is teaching in a university or college, tomorrow's lecture allows a second opportunity to repeat the basic ideas. With a book, the problem is more difficult, since some readers skip the concluding chapter and other readers (maybe those accustomed to reading mystery novels) automatically read the conclusion first and then decide whether to finish the book.

My objectives in this concluding chapter are to summarize the text's primary bankruptcy lessons and to evaluate bankruptcy within an overall strategic perspective. (Hopefully, mystery readers will be intrigued and will turn next to chapter 1.) This conclusion will give readers who have already finished the book both a review of the major ideas and an appreciation of the role of bankruptcy in corporate finance.

The Lessons of Bankruptcy

Bankruptcy may affect any business. In the corporate taxonomy developed in chapter 1, there are four types of firms distinguishable by their product and financial condition. Eagles have healthy products and finances, tortoises have weak products, condors have weak finances, and dinosaurs have weak products and finances. By definition, every bankrupt firm is a dinosaur. Condors and tortoises may be transformed into dinosaurs if their healthy aspect weakens. Even eagles may falter if both product and financial conditions worsen.

Why Companies Fail focuses on financial reasons for failure. There are five common bankruptcy traps: the cash-flow cycle, excessive current assets, an overabundance of fixed assets, a shortage of capital, and a reliance on short-term debt. The five traps threaten every business and may cause even the best firms to stumble.

There is no way to guarantee that a company's managers will discover an impending trap before it harms their company. Arguably, the methods of bankruptcy detection presented in chapter 8 may enable some firms to act before it is too late. Every company's financial managers and owners must remain vigilant against financial failure, constantly checking and comparing a firm's performance against other firms in the same industry and against its own historic performance.

There is no need to panic if you should discover that your firm is on the verge of failing. First, consider the following thought: you are not alone. Probably many of your customers and suppliers (whether they know it or not) are in the same situation. Second, realize that some failing firms will survive. Moreover, some of the failing firms might have survived had their managers attempted company-saving strategies like those described in chapter 9. Before conceding defeat, be sure to review all your options.

Investing in bankrupt companies has become an accepted, if not a recommended, strategy. Before participating in such a plan, reread chapter 10 and consider how often an eagle can be created out of a dinosaur. If you do invest in bankrupt companies, spread your assets out in a portfolio and consider buying bonds instead of stocks.

The Strategic Use of Bankruptcy

The "bankruptcy is comparable to death" metaphor that pervades the first ten chapters is only partially correct. There is another side to the coin: bankruptcy also has the power to give life to dying companies. In some cases, bankruptcy extends a company's life by forcing creditors and owners to settle previous obligations and to reorganize the firm into a healthier enterprise. In other cases, bankruptcy gives life when a company threatens to file for bankruptcy court protection and is then given extra time to put its affairs in order by creditors who want to keep the matter out of court.

When a company files under the bankruptcy act for protection from creditors, it generally is given time to develop a plan of reorganization. When a dinosaur is reorganized after receiving the court's protection, a healthier enterprise may emerge. Both financial and product changes are implemented to correct problems that led to the original crisis. Court protection provides a grace period from creditors' ceaseless demands for payment. Without this hiatus, failing companies might be seized by creditors who would hope to dispose of assets speedily in order to settle claims.

In a liquidation, creditors may not fully recover their capital. Losses are especially common among holders of unsecured debt, who must wait to recover their capital until after the full repayment of secured creditors.

In both reorganizations and liquidations, similar percentage settlements are offered to most classes of creditors; however, in the interest of equity, it is possible that certain creditors may obtain extra payments in a reorganization.

The knowledge that most eventual claim settlements following a filing in bankruptcy court return only cents on the dollar gives the threat of bankruptcy great leverage for the manager of a troubled firm. By threatening to file court papers, the manager may forestall creditor actions that would harm the firm's chances to recover. But if creditors believe that the current management team is incapable of solving any problems, the threat may have little strength.

Companies should be careful not to use the threat of bankruptcy needlessly. If they do, they will acquire a reputation as either an impending failure or as a company that attempts to not pay its bills. Lenders will avoid the firm. A bad reputation may take a long time to be forgotten.

Bankruptcy is thus a source of life and death. It has powers to heal and renew to the same extent as it connotates corporate extinction. In fact, recent developments (Continental Airlines, Manville, and others) suggest that in the future, bankruptcy will be even more prominent, extending its influence into nontraditional areas.

Appendix A
The Failure Record

The first bankruptcy probably occurred not long after the formation of the first business. Yet scientific interest in the subject was not awakened until the Great Depression. One of the earliest analyses was prepared in 1935 by R. Smith and A. Winakor when they examined the capital structure of unsuccessful companies.[1] Other research soon followed, and today the subject of bankruptcy is widely discussed and researched.

Bankruptcy research has taken two directions. The first investigates the determinants of macro or national failure rates. Although major research in this area is limited, it includes studies by Noto and Zimmerman, Altman, and Platt.[2] The remainder of this chapter is devoted to an overview of this topic area.

The second category of bankruptcy studies are micro or firm-specific studies, which attempt to uncover a set of variables capable of predicting future bankruptcies. Chapter 8 in this book describes several of these studies and discusses their usefulness and general findings.

Good research requires good data. Macrobankruptcy studies have tended to rely heavily on the information gathered and disseminated by the Dun & Bradstreet Corporation (D&B). D&B bankruptcy reports include the annual publication *The Dun & Bradstreet Business Failure Record* and the *Quarterly Failure Report*. When a firm in an industry covered by D&B goes out of business, it is classified as a business failure if any of the following conditions is met:

The firm has gone bankrupt.

The firm's assets have been assigned (given) to creditors.

The firm has been reorganized.

The firm has terminated business without fully satisfying all creditor's claim.

Table A–1
Failures since 1925

Year	Number of Failures	Failures per 10,000 Firms
1925	21,214	100
1926	21,773	101
1927	23,146	106
1928	23,842	109
1929	22,909	104
1930	26,355	122
1931	28,285	133
1932	31,822	154
1933	19,859	100
1934	12,091	61
1935	12,244	62
1936	9,607	48
1937	9,490	46
1938	12,836	61
1939	14,768	70
1940	13,619	63
1941	11,848	55
1942	9,405	45
1943	3,221	16
1944	1,222	7
1945	809	4
1946	1,129	5
1947	3,474	14
1948	5,250	20
1949	9,246	34
1950	9,162	34
1951	8,058	31
1952	7,611	29
1953	8,862	33
1954	11,086	42
1955	10,969	42
1956	12,686	48
1957	13,739	52
1958	14,964	56
1959	14,053	52
1960	15,445	57
1961	17,075	64
1962	15,782	61
1963	14,374	56
1964	13,501	53
1965	13,514	53
1966	13,061	52
1967	12,364	49
1968	9,636	39
1960	9,154	37
1970	10,748	44
1971	10,326	42
1972	9,566	38
1973	9,345	36
1974	9,915	38
1975	11,432	43

Table A–1 continued

Year	Number of Failures	Failures per 10,000 Firms
1976	9,628	35
1977	7,919	28
1978	6,619	24
1979	7,564	28
1980	11,742	42
1981	16,794	61
1982	25,346	89[a]

Source: *The 1981 Dun & Bradstreet Business Failure Record,* used with permission.
[a]Preliminary estimate.

Although the D&B data are the best information available, they do not include all industries. Omitted are failures in the financial sector and among real estate firms.

National Failure Rates

D&B has popularized the use of failure rates. *Failure rates* translate raw failure numbers into ratios by dividing the number of failures by the number of firms. They are more meaningful than the number of annual failures since the ratio calculates the percentage of firms failing. Table A–1 lists the number of national failures and the failure rate per 10,000 firms for the period 1925 through 1982.

The failure rate of 100 in 1925 indicates that in that year, 100 out of every 10,000 firms failed. By contrast, in 1981, only 61 out of every 10,000 firms failed. The failure rate rises and falls in a cyclical pattern that mirrors changes in both the health of the national economy and the rate of formation of new corporations, the two economic phenomena that underlie the failure rate. Corporate profits are strong in a robust economy. Profits and failures are negatively correlated since unprofitable firms are failure prone. Thus the failure rate declines when the economy is healthy.

A healthy economy also induces individuals to create new business enterprises. Newer firms, however, have higher failure rates than established enterprises. For example, in 1981, approximately 23 percent of firms had been formed within the past three years and an additional 26 percent of failing firms were either four or five years old.[3] Only 20 percent of failing firms had been in existence for at least ten years. Therefore a strong economy affects the failure rate in two ways. First, the failure rate falls as corporate profits respond to economic growth. Second, the rate of failure increases as new firms, with a higher incidence of failure, are created.

The worst year for business failures was 1932, in the midst of the depression. Interestingly the failure rate was high and quite close to the record value in the seven years preceding 1932. In no year since 1932 has the failure rate reached levels anywhere near values observed in the period 1925 through 1929. The years 1925 through 1929 were go-go years. Enterprise and the spirit of adventure pervaded the United States. Everyone was out to get rich quick. The environment was conducive to risk taking; that is, high profits stimulated the rate of business formation. Since new businesses are more likely to fail than old firms, the failure rate was high throughout the period.

Preliminary information shows that 1982 appears to have had the highest annual failure rate since 1933. Not only that, but more firms failed in 1982 than failed in 1929, the first year of the Great Depression. Two factors are probably responsible for 1982's high failure rate. First, in the years immediately preceding 1982, the U.S. economy was weak, experiencing two back-to-back recessions. Failures typically increase several quarters after the commencement of recessions. Second, President Ronald Reagan's tax law modifications provided incentives to entrepreneurs to strike out on their own. Some of these people created businesses that failed in 1982. The experience is similar to that found in the 1925 through 1928 period.

The lowest percentage rate of failure occurred in 1945 during World War II. There were 97 percent fewer failures in 1945 than in 1932. The failure rate was low throughout the war years and did not return to normal levels until about 1949. Probably the most salient conclusion is that failure is costly. When a firm fails, productive resources are tied up for an indefinite period of time, and bankruptcy services are demanded and taken from other uses. In a war period, resources cannot be wasted, and thus bankruptcy filings must be curtailed. Moreover, with so many persons involved in military activities and with no funds available to build new nonessential enterprises, remaining civilians and existing businesses earn above-normal wages and profits. Thus, fewer failures result from economic causes.

Failure rates might be viewed by decade, as shown in table A–2. Except for the unusual experience during World War II, it is possible to discern a steady decline in the business failure rate. Probably the two most salient factors leading to the decline are the effects of increased management of economic cycles by the federal government and the increase in industrial concentration (how large an industry's four largest firms are relative to the other firms).

One product of the depression era was a tremendous increase in the study of economic behavior. The economist and his or her model left the halls of academia and entered the world of politics. Stabilization policy

Table A–2
Average Failure Rates by Decade

Decade	Average Failure Rate
1925–1929	104
1930–1939	60
1940–1949	26
1950–1951	42
1960–1969	52
1970–1979	36

became accepted practice. With *stabilization policy,* the government attempts to regulate the amount of economic activity by varying spending and tax policies and the amount of money in circulation. Despite the current debate over the merits of activist economic policies, the past four decades have witnessed fewer and less severe economic recessions than in previous decades. As a result, the business failure rate is now, on average, lower than it has ever been.

The past thirty years have also witnessed a move toward greater industrial concentration. Economists generally measure industrial concentration by determining the proportion of an industry's sales made by the largest firms in the industry. By this measure, the concentration of U.S. business is rising; however, while larger firms are becoming more important contributors in their own industry, the total number of firms in most industries is not falling. Table A–3 documents the overall in-

Table A–3
Number of Firms in 1950 and 1980 by Industry

Industry	Number of Firms		Percentage Change
	1950	1980	
Mining	27,634	29,676	7.4
Food	37,699	20,983	(44.4)
Textiles	40,882	28,369	(30.7)
Lumber	46,193	38,603	(16.5)
Paper	35,558	50,990	43.4
Chemicals	11,211	11,261	0.4
Leather	5,227	2,626	(49.8)
Stone	10,809	15,645	44.7
Metals	23,667	38,232	61.5
Machinery	23,486	60,000	155.5
Transportation	4,257	8,369	96.6
Miscellaneous manufacturing	19,219	27,407	42.6
Retail	1,010,815	1,222,928	21.0
Wholesale	236,278	384,833	62.9
Construction	248,170	417,953	68.4
Commercial services	722,203	1,566,325	116.9

Source: U.S. Bureau of the Census, *County Business Patterns.*

crease in the number of firms. Only four of sixteen industries experienced falling numbers of firms between 1950 and 1980. Yet rising industrial concentration may still contribute to falling business failure rates. Specifically, if more concentrated industries have more stable price levels (fewer price wars and fewer periods of insufficient supply), there may then be less pressure on the firms in the industry and concomitantly fewer failures.

Industry Failure Rates

The failure rate experience varies across industries. Nationally the failure rate is declining over time, despite a slight increase in the rate of failure during the 1960s. Industry-specific data present a slightly different story. Table A–4 presents average failure rates by industry over a decade. On an industry-specific basis, different trends are observed. For example, the food, textiles, leather, stone, clay, and glass industries did not experience a higher failure rate in the 1960s. Instead, their failure rates declined steadily from 1950 onward. The mining, metals, transportation equipment, construction, and commercial services industries had greater failure rates during the 1970s than during the 1950s.

Table A–4
Average Failure Rate by Industry

	Average Failure Rate			
Industry	1950s	1960s	1970s	1950–1982
Mining	34	71	43	58
Food	126	107	86	105
Textiles	288	274	200	240
Lumber	189	234	118	172
Paper	84	123	103	104
Chemicals	116	160	114	127
Leather	421	371	237	309
Stone	99	95	70	90
Metals	79	117	86	99
Machinery	178	180	126	155
Transportation	246	398	255	291
Miscellaneous manufacturing	398	493	270	372
Retail	107	161	96	120
Wholesale	88	124	74	96
Construction	103	199	116	142
Commercial services	22	33	27	28

Source: Derived from Dun & Bradstreet Corporation, *Quarterly Failure Record*, and U.S. Bureau of the Census, *County Business Patterns*.

Note: Number of failures per 100,000 firms.

The steady decline in the business failure rate in the food, textiles, leather, and stone industries is probably a result of more stable price levels caused by increased industrial concentration. Three of the four industries ended the period with fewer total firms than were in existence in 1950. Moreover, once the weaker firms in an industry vacate, the failure rate will decline unless new, weak firms enter the industry. These four industries have not witnessed substantial new firm formation in recent years.

In the case of the five industries with higher average failures in the 1970s than in the 1950s, several forces are probably responsible. The metals and transportation equipment industries have faced intense international competition over this period. Weaker firms have succumbed to heightened competition. The mining industry is feeling the effect of bouncing energy prices. First, prices rise, and new firms are formed. Then energy prices fall, and marginal producers fail. If energy prices become more stable in the late 1980s, this phenomenon may be reversed. Construction has felt the effects of interest rate volatility. Like the mining industry, when interest rates fall and construction activity increases, marginal firms enter the business. Higher interest rates reduce activity overall but more so for new, less well-known firms. These firms fail when the high rates persist. If the late 1980s have less interest rate volatility than the previous three decades, the failure rate of the construction industry may begin to decline.

A second consequence of smaller swings between recessions and booms in the economy has been a decrease in the volatility of industry failure rates. Volatility, which is usually measured by variance, calculates by how much annual and average failure rates differ. When each annual failure rate is exactly equal to the average failure rate, the variance of that industry's failure rate equals zero. By contrast, when annual failure rates are all quite different from the average failure rate, the industry failure rate has a high variance. For each of sixteen industries, table A–5 lists failure rate variances for the three decades beginning with 1950. The evidence supports the notion that over time industry failure rates have been converging toward their industry's average failure rate.

Thirteen of the sixteen industries in table A–5 have experienced lower failure variances; these industries are approaching a state in which annual failures, as a percentage of total firms, tend not to change radically year after year. Since bankruptcy imposes significant costs on both individuals and society, falling failure rates and smaller failure variances are positive developments.

Three industries—mining, paper, and chemicals—had higher failure variances in the 1970s than during the 1950s. The increases in the paper

Table A–5
Variance of Industry Failure Rates

Industry	Failure Variance			
	1950s	1960s	1970s	1950–1982
Mining	4	3	15	21
Food	11	4	4	10
Textiles	65	41	28	62
Lumber	47	33	9	55
Paper	3	5	6	12
Chemicals	14	18	18	23
Leather	177	161	91	230
Stone	20	10	6	18
Metals	14	9	4	17
Machinery	48	18	17	37
Transportation	130	139	111	171
Miscellaneous manufacturing	110	79	86	196
Retail	26	5	2	20
Wholesale	16	3	1	13
Construction	29	6	8	46
Commercial services	1	0	0	1

Source: Derived from Dun & Bradstreet Corporation, *Quarterly Failure Record*, and U.S. Bureau of the Census, *County Business Patterns*.
Note: Data are multiplied by 1,000 because of small size.

and chemical industries are minor. The mining increase is large but is mostly due to an external event, the Arab oil embargo and higher energy prices, not likely to be repeated. Thus, the three nontypical industries do not appear to pose worrisome problems.

The failure variances of the transportation equipment industry have tended to be significantly higher than average by a factor of five to ten over the entire period 1950 through 1982. This demonstrates the relationship between economic prosperity and failure in an industry. Autos are a durable good mostly purchased by the household sector. When the economy slumps or interest rates rise, individuals immediately delay planned auto purchases. Industry activity slows down, and business failures occur. As the economy rebounds, the industry recovers, and fewer failures occur. There is a tremendous difference between the failure rate in good years and bad years, and thus the variance is high.

Why Firms Failed in 1981

One of the most fascinating sections of *The Dun & Bradstreet Business Failure Record* is a table that indicates why businesses fail. Table A–6 summarizes the report on failures in 1981. Each of the top four entries

Table A-6
Why 16,794 Businesses Failed in 1981

Reason	Percentage
Inadequate line experience	11.1
Inadequate managerial experience	12.5
Unbalanced experience	19.2
Incompetence	45.6
Other	1.5
Unknown	10.1

Source: *The 1981 Dun & Bradstreet Business Failure Record*, used with permission.

in the table provides the same message: too many firms fail because their managers are inadequately trained and lack sufficient experience. Critics of graduate business education programs, as well as critics of the popularization of management education in best-selling books, videotapes, and lecture series, should consider the consequence of managers with too little training: the firms they run fail. Perhaps another reason why the national business failure rate has been declining since 1929 is that more business managers are receiving formal business training.

Dun & Bradstreet actually goes one step further in its analysis: it attempts to identify the apparent causes of failure. For the top four categories listed in table A-6, the causes of failure are presented in table A-7.

Table A-7
Causes of Most Failures
(percentages)

Cause	Manufacturing	Wholesale	Retail	Construction	Commercial Services
Inadequate Sales	58	59	61	64	50
Heavy operating expense	33	26	22	22	30
Receivables difficulties	12	12	2	9	5
Inventory difficulties	5	11	12	1	1
Excess fixed assets	5	2	3	2	6
Poor location	1	1	4	1	2
Competitive weakness	15	17	18	15	16

Source: *The 1981 Dun & Bradstreet Failure Record*, used with permission.
Note: Totals may exceed 100 percent because some failures are due to several causes.

Each of the five bankruptcy-creating errors discussed in chapters 3 through 7 of this book is a prominent element in table A–7. This means that many companies, not only those highlighted in this book, have bankruptcy problems resulting from getting caught in the cash-flow cycle, buried under assets, squeezed by equipment, lost with too little capital, and pinched by short-term debt. The information in table A–7 is remarkably stable across industries. For example, between 50 and 60 percent of bankruptcies in every industry are at least partially due to inadequate sales. Moreover, between 22 and 32 percent of bankruptcies in every industry occur in firms with too-heavy operating expenses. This implies that the same set of mistakes is made and remade.

Appendix B
Basic Accounting for
Nonfinancial Readers

For the benefit of readers unable to distinguish an income statement from a balance sheet, this chapter presents a short and simple overview of basic accounting principles. The sole purpose is to help readers gain more from the chapters. Many readers can probably skim or completely omit this appendix. Those who want a more detailed review of accounting are referred to Robert Anthony's *Fundamentals of Accounting*.

Every publicly held company is required by law to produce two annual reports. One report, the 10-K, is submitted to the Securities and Exchange Commission (SEC) and is available to the public through government depository libraries or on request from the company. The second annual report is prepared for distribution to shareholders. The 10-K report contains more comprehensive and detailed information than does the shareholders' report. Thus, it is advisable to read the 10-K even though it is more difficult to obtain.

The 10-K report contains the following information:

Financial data (including the annual report, balance sheet, and changes in financial position).

A discussion by management of where the company has been and where it is going, both operationally as well as financially.

Disclosure of significant facts such as law suits or corporate investments.

Names and addresses of key employees.

Unless you speak the language of accounting, you will have trouble understanding the 10-K and perceiving how a company has gotten itself into financial difficulties. Therefore, let us proceed to the accounting review.

Accounting Review

The two most important accounting reports are the income statement and the balance sheet. An *income statement* shows how much money a company lost or made during a specified period of time, normally a quarter or a year. The *balance sheet* records a firm's assets and liabilities. Let us start by reviewing the income statement.

Financial reports are more readable when real numbers are used. I have chosen the financial statements in Prime Computer's 1983 annual report to use as an example. According to the information in table B–1, Prime Computer had total revenue of approximately $516 million from the sale of computers and computer services in 1983. Before we turn to the Prime report, one or two words of caution are in order. Without looking further into Prime's annual report, I cannot tell you exactly what this dollar figure means. Companies may choose several methods to "book" revenue. Some firms book revenue when a sale is made; more conservative firms book revenue when the product is literally carried out the factory door; still more conservative companies wait for the customer to receive the product before recording a sale. The more conservative the accounting practice, the less likely are unpleasant surprises. (In late 1984, for example, the SEC accused Stauffer Chemical of prematurely booking revenue. The company chose to settle the dispute rather than fight the SEC. By settling, the company agreed to be a little less aggressive in calculating sales.)

A second uncertainty relating to revenue has to do with when the company actually obtains its money. Let us imagine a computer that Prime Computer might have sold in 1983 to a company. By the time the machine reached the company, Prime will have recorded a sale, but it will probably not have received any cash money since most goods are sold with credit terms giving the consumer several days or weeks in which to pay. (In the balance sheet section, we will see that credit extended to

Table B–1
Prime Computer's 1983 Income Statement[a]
(thousands of dollars)

Total revenue	$516,503
Costs and expenses	465,538
Operating income	50,965
Interest and other expense	3,168
Income before tax	47,797
Taxes	15,294
Net income	$ 32,503

[a]Slightly adjusted.

customers is recorded on the balance sheet as an account receivable.) Large companies may have finance subsidiaries to help cutomers pay for expensive capital goods in the same way consumers might charge purchases at a department store. If not, the customer may go to a bank to borrow the funds, or if the firm has ample cash reserves, it may be able to finance the purchase on its own. However the money is obtained, at some point in the future, normally in about thirty days, Prime receives payment for its computer.

For a discussion of failures and bankruptcies such as ours, two important implications arise from the use of credit. First, Prime Computer will normally collect some 1983 sales dollars in 1984, some first-quarter sales in the second quarter, and so on. This delayed-payment phenomenon is part of the cash-flow cycle. It is often mentioned as a common cause of business failure. A solution is not to stop offering credit, since credit is offered as a way to generate more sales; instead, the firm needs to plan ahead and must be ready to deal with the cash-flow cycle.

Second, if credit has been extended to a firm that went bankrupt, actual revenue will be less than recorded revenue since it is unlikely that the bankrupt will pay this credit soon. Firms account for nonpayment of recorded revenues by taking a bad debt expense against current revenues; that is, they recognize that the funds will never be collected. Normally the proportion of past sales lost to bad debts is less than 1 or 2 percent. In special circumstances, however, as in the case of a depressed industry (for example, semiconductors in 1979, oil field equipment in 1983, and microcomputers in 1984), sizable past revenues may need to be written off when borrowers start to fail.

One bankruptcy may cause other bankruptcies if the failing firm is sufficiently large with many sizable trade creditors. For example, Chrysler might have caused a cascade of additional bankruptcies had the company not been bailed out of its financial difficulties by a federal loan guarantee. There is arguably no other rationale available to justify governmental antibankruptcy intervention. (Though the outcome and eventual financial ramifications of the Federal Deposit Insurance Corporation's (FDIC) bailout of Continental Illinois Bank is not yet known, the failure of a wholesale bank the size of Continental would certainly have wreaked havoc on the economy. Bankruptcy specialists, investors, and legislators are most interested in the amount of suffering imposed on shareholders by the FDIC. If shareholders absorb most of the risk associated with stockownership, then the bailout will probably get high marks.)

Prime Computer had operating income of approximately $50.9 million in 1983, as shown in table B–1. Operating income equals the difference between total revenue and all costs except the costs associated with financing the business. Costs not deducted to get to operating income include interest, preferred stock dividends, and common stock dividends. Bankrupt companies intent on reorganization receiving court protection from creditors (Chapter 11 bankruptcy) suspend interest and dividend payments on old debt. Thus, operating income is the same as net income in the financial report of a bankrupt company. Nonbankrupt firms, making interest and dividends payments, lower operating income by these amounts plus their income tax payments to get net income. In 1983, Prime earned over $32 million after taxes.

Because firms in Chapter 11 halt interest and dividend payments, they often report a profit while they are still under the protection of bankruptcy courts. While some investors are encouraged by the rapid return to profitability, it is better not to get too carried away by the reported profits since the bankrupt firm is not reporting all its costs. In fact, if the bankruptcy resulted from financial causes rather than operating problems, there may have always been operating profits.

Net income is often reported as *earnings per share* (EPS). This measure spreads the income over the common stock outstanding and tells how much profit has been earned for each share. Prime Computer had 47.8 million common shares, so in 1983 it earned $0.68 per share.

What does a company do with its after-tax income? Essentially there are two choices: earnings can be paid out as dividends or be retained by the corporation. Retained earnings are not converted into thousand dollar bills and then stacked in the company president's office but are used to support new investment in plant, equipment, research, and so forth. Retained earnings are a good alternative to obtaining money with bank loans or from the sale of new common stock. Companies with fewer investment opportunities, usually those in older, more established industries, tend to pay dividends, while newer firms usually reinvest their net income and retain their earnings.

Table B–2 presents Prime Computer's balance sheet in 1983. I have simplified it so as to highlight its essential parts. It is important to observe that the balance sheet is not only conceptually different from the income statement but that it also has a time difference. A balance sheet examines a company at one exact moment in time—for example, midnight on December 31—while the income statement looks across time over a quarter or a year.

The time difference between the two relates to the conceptual purposes of the two financial reports. The balance sheet reports on a firm's financial health, and thus it must pinpoint the diagnosis to an exact moment. In contrast, the income statement reports a firm's profit or loss for a period of time; in essence, it reviews the firm's operating health.

Table B–2
Prime Computer's 1983 Balance Sheet[a]
(thousands of dollars)

Assets		Liabilities and Net Worth	
Current assets		Current liabilities	
Cash	$ 45,069	Bank loans	$ 5,645
Accounts receivable	161,139	Trade credit	40,985
less allowance for		Other liabilities	49,380
doubtful accounts			96,010
Inventory	85,219		
Other assets	7,548		
	298,975		
Long-term assets		Long-term liabilities	
Land and buildings	51,995	Taxes owed	64,272
Equipment	146,070	Bond due in 1992	10,000
Less accumulated		Capital lease	
depreciation	52,300	obligation	6,279
	145,765	Net worth	80,551
		Money raised from	
		sale of stock	98,327
		Accumulated	
		retained earnings	169,852
Total	$444,740	Total	$444,740

[a]Slightly adjusted.

By way of analogy, imagine you were taking an automobile trip. At the end of the day you sit down and prepare both a balance sheet and an income statement. Your income statement might report that you drove 575 miles and spent $73.15 out of pocket that day (just as profits earned during a time period summarizes a firm's achievements). Both miles driven and cash spent refer to your accomplishments in a specific day. Your balance sheet might report, on the other hand, you were now in Omaha, Nebraska, with $141.15 in your pocket and 600 miles to go until you reach the end of your journey. Thus, the balance sheet describes your current status as of now. The same can be said of a company's balance sheet.

As in table B–2, companies always show a balance between their assets on the one hand and their liabilities and net worth on the other hand. In the case of Prime Computer, both the left- and right-hand sides of the balance sheet total $444.7 million. This balance is always maintained since, as shown in chapter 1 for Texas International Company, if the value of book assets exceeds total liabilities, net worth is reported as being negative. Net worth therefore exactly equals the difference between a company's assets and liabilities.

Both assets and liabilities are divided into two parts: current (meaning due or convertible into cash within the next 12 months) and long term. The distinction between the two is important. Current assets and liabilities pose immediate concerns; after all, technical insolvency is defined as having insufficient current assets to meet current liabilities. Current liabilities and their relation to the firm's cash flow are one of the best predictors of failure. Long-term assets and liabilities are less liquid, less problematic, and less often radically changed.

Table B–3
Balance Sheet Terms

Term	Definition	Corporate Purpose
Cash	Money, possibly marketable securities ties, held by firm	To pay bills and maintain liquidity
Accounts receivable	Credit extended to customers	In many industries, a necessary part of doing business
Inventory	Raw materials, goods being produced, and finished goods not yet sold	Required investment in order to have a product to sell
Depreciation	Dollars expensed against income to reflect the deterioration and wear and tear on capital goods and buildings	Lowers income taxes and raises flow, thereby allowing firm to buy new assets
Bank loans	Often called *notes payable*; short-term credit extended by a bank	Usually to meet short-term needs
Trade credit	Often called *accounts payable*; money or credit extended by a supplier	See *Accounts receivable*
Bond	A corporate IOU often sold to public	Usually raised for long-term investments
Capital lease	Value of lease obligations on land, buildings, and equipment over three-year leases	An alternative to debt
Retained earnings	Profits not paid as dividends over the firm's history	Funds used to purchase assets, not raised by selling stock or debt

Each item listed beneath current and long-term assets and liabilities in table B–2 is important, and its definition and corporate meaning ought to be understood. Not only do these terms appear throughout this book, but by incorporating them in your business discussions, you can increase the objectivity and precision of your remarks. Table B–3 explains these concepts.

Table B–2 shows that Prime has approximately $299 million in current assets and $146 million in long-term assets. Prime's liabilities equal approximately $177 million, of which $96 million is current liabilities. Net worth of about $268 million is divided into $98 million raised by selling stock and $170 million accumulated from prior earnings. Where has this $170 million gone? Prime used this money to buy assets to enable growth. Hence, the money is seen on the left-hand side as assets and on the right-hand side as liabilities. Accumulated profits are not stored in the chairperson's office as a stack of money.

Two relatively easy methods to assess a firm's financial health are carried out using balance sheet data. First, available working capital is calculated by subtracting current liabilities from current assets. Prime has $203 million in working capital. These are the funds available for growth. Second, dividing total liabilities by total assets gives the debt-to-asset ratio. Prime's ratio is 0.40, which is higher than that of the average firm, 0.33. This calculation reveals that Prime uses more debt than the typical U.S. firm though the average debt-to-asset ratio in the computer industry may be higher than is typical for the average firm.

Notes

Chapter 3
Getting Caught in the Cash-Flow Cycle

1. Lionel Corporation, *Interim Report* (April 28, 1984).

Chapter 6
Getting Lost with Too-Little Capital

1. *New York Times*, August 19, 1984.
2. Ibid.

Chapter 7
Getting Pinched by Short-Term Debt

1. *Business Week*, November 21, 1983.

Chapter 8
Detecting Future Bankruptcies

1. E.I. Altman, *Corporate Financial Distress* (New York: Wiley, 1983), p. 254.
2. Among these theorists are E.I. Altman, W. Beaver, and R.O. Edmister.
3. See, for example, J.F. Weston and E.F. Brigham, *Managerial Finance*, 7th ed. (New York: Dryden Press, 1981); R. Moyer, J. McGuigan, and W. Kretlow, *Contemporary Financial Management*, 2d ed. (Minneapolis: West Publishing Co., 1984); Benton Gup, *Principles of Financial Management* (New York: Wiley, 1983).
4. E.I. Altman, "Financial Ratios, Discriminant Analysis and the Prediction of Corporate Bankruptcy," *Journal of Finance* (September 1968); E.I. Altman, R. Haldeman, and P. Narayanan, "Zeta Analysis: A New Model to Identify Bank-

ruptcy Risk of Corporations," *Journal of Banking and Finance* (June 1977); C. Pantalone and M.A. Platt, "Savings and Loan Failures: A Discriminate Analysis," working paper, Northeastern University (1985).

5. Altman, "Financial Ratios."
6. Altman, Haldeman, and Narayanan, "Zeta Analysis."
7. Pantalone and Platt, "Savings and Loan Failures."

Chapter 9
Strategies for the Near-Bankrupt

1. *Wall Street Journal*, October 30, 1984.

Appendix A
The Failure Record

1. R. Smith and A. Winakor, *Changes in Financial Structure of Unsuccessful Corporations* (Urbana: University of Illinois, Bureau of Business Research, 1935).

2. N. Noto and D. Zimmerman, "A Comparison of Failure and Liability Trends in Manufacturing and Nonmanufacturing Industries: Implications for Business" (Washington, D.C.: Congressional Research Services, January 1981); E.I. Altman, *Corporate Financial Distress* (New York: Wiley, 1983); H.D. Platt, "Interindustry Bankruptcy: Detecting the Causal Ordering of Corporate Failure," working paper, Northeastern University (1985).

3. Dun & Bradstreet, *Business Failure Record 1981* (New York: Dun & Bradstreet, 1983).

Glossary

Arrearage   Overdue payment such as an omitted dividend.

Assignment   Transference of ownership in an asset from a debtor to a creditor; a technique that is used to release debtor from an obligation while minimizing court costs.

Bankruptcy   Having liabilities in excess of assets.

Bond   A corporate IOU.

Book Value   The value of an asset on a company's balance sheet. Since the balance sheet reflects accumulated depreciation, book value may or may not have any relationship to actual value.

Break-even Analysis   The determination of the sales quantity required to cover operating expenses.

Cash-Flow Coverage   The ability of funds flowing in to pay upcoming obligations.

Capital   Money or funds available.

Capital Structure   The composition of a firm's liabilities. It summarizes the debt-equity choice.

Collateral   Assets used to secure a loan.

Common Stock   Shares owning the firm and eligible to vote and receive dividends.

Composition   The reduction of the face amount of a debtor's obligation. Normally, in exchange for this concession, the creditor is compensated with stock warrants or convertible debt.

Convertible Debt   Debt that may be converted into a different asset. In some cases, debt is convertible into stock, oil, or silver.

Covenant   The contractual terms defining the relationship between a creditor and debtor. For example, the debtor may be allowed to redeem debt whenever it wishes.

Cumulative Dividends   Dividends that, if not paid, become an obligation of the firm. Normally they are repaid in the future, when the creditor's circumstances improve.

Current Ratio   The ratio of current assets to current liabilities.

Debenture   An unsecured bond.

Debt Ratio   Total debt divided by total assets.

EBIT   Operating income.

Equity   A company's net worth. Includes the money paid by original investors for stock and accumulated retained earnings.

Extension   The process permitting a debtor to delay repayment of either interest or principal.

Financial Leverage   The percentage impact on net income of a percentage change in operating income. Firms using high levels of debt have higher financial leverage.

Fixed Cost   Costs that do not vary as output is changed. For example, mortgage payments will not change if a factory doubles its output.

Income Bond   A bond that pays interest only in years a company earns an income.

Indenture   The formal agreement between debtors and creditors containing the covenants.

Insolvency   Current liabilities in excess of current assets.

Lien   A charge on an asset for the repayment of a debt.

Margin   The percentage of net income to sales.

Net Income   Revenue less all costs; not included are dividends paid to common stock.

Operating Income or Profit   Revenue less operating expenses; not included are interest and other financial costs and taxes.

Operating Leverage   The percentage impact on operating income of a percentage change in sales. Capital-intensive industries have higher operating leverage.

Opportunity Cost   The value of resources in other better uses.

Perpetual Bond   A bond that pays interest forever but is never redeemed.

Preferred Stock   Stock that receives a fixed dividend payment and normally is not eligible to vote.

Principal   The amount of a loan remaining to be repaid.

Prospectus   Information given to potential buyers by the seller of a new security.

Redemption   The repayment of principal by a debtor.

Reorganization   The process, the reverse of bankruptcy, wherein a troubled firm survives. Normally, the balance sheet restates the value of assets to reflect their true value, and liabilities and net worth undergo corresponding changes.

Retained Earnings   Net income less dividends paid to common stock.

Secured Bond   A bond backed by some real asset. For example, a mortgage bond is secured by a piece of real property.

Sinking Fund   A fund, earning interest, to be used to redeem debt. The establishment of a sinking fund reduces the risk that a debtor will never repay a debt.

Subordinated Debenture   An unsecured bond eligible for repayment in a reorganization or bankruptcy only after a more senior debt is repaid.

Time Factor   The time elapsing between the decision to produce a good and when funds are actually received by the producer.

Warrant   A long-term stock option.

Working Capital   The difference between current assets and current liabilities.

Bibliography

Altman, E.I. "Financial Ratios, Discriminant Analysis and the Prediction of Corporate Bankruptcy." *Journal of Finance* (September 1968).

——— . *Corporate Financial Distress*. New York: Wiley, 1983.

Altman, E.I., R. Haldeman, and P. Narayanan. "Zeta Analysis: A New Model to Identify Bankruptcy Risk of Corporations." *Journal of Banking and Finance* (June 1977).

Anthony, R.N. *Fundamentals of Accounting*. New York: Irwin, 1984.

Archibald, R., and S. Baker. "A Model of Aggregate Business Failure." Unpublished manuscript, College of William and Mary, 1984.

Beaver, W. "Financial Ratios as Predictors of Failures." *Journal of Accounting Research* (January 1967).

Deakin, E.B. "A Discriminant Analysis of Predictors of Business Failures." *Journal of Accounting Research* (March 1972).

Dun & Bradstreet. *Business Failure Record 1981*. New York: Dun & Bradstreet, 1983.

Ibbotson, R.G., and R.A. Sinquefield. *Stocks, Bonds, Bills and Inflation: The Past and the Future*. New York: Financial Analysts Research Foundation, 1982.

Moyer, R., J. McGuigan, and W. Kretlow. *Contemporary Financial Management*. 2d ed. Minneapolis: West Publishing Co., 1984.

Noto, N., and D. Zimmerman. "A Comparison of Failure and Liability Trends in Manufacturing and Nonmanufacturing Industries: Implications for Business." Washington, D.C.: Congressional Research Service, January 1981.

Pantalone, C., and M.A. Platt. "Savings and Loan Failures: A Discriminate Analysis." Working paper, Northeastern University, 1985.

——— . "Understanding the Causes of Differential Commercial Bank and Savings and Loan Failures." Working paper, Northeastern University, 1985.

Platt, H.D. "Interindustry Bankruptcy: Detecting the Causal Ordering of Corporate Failure." Working paper, Northeastern University, 1985.

Platt, H.D. "Tax Climate Effects on Interindustry Bankruptcy." Working paper, Northeastern University, 1985.

Smith, R., and A. Winakor. *Changes in Financial Structure of Unsuccessful Corporations*. Urbana: University of Illinois, Bureau of Business Research, 1935.

U.S. Department of Commerce, Bureau of Census. *County Business Patterns*. Annual (except 1954 and 1955).

Weston, J.F., and E.F. Brigham. *Managerial Finance*. 7th ed. Dryden Press, 1981.
Wilcox, J.W. "A Gambler's Ruin Prediction of Business Failure Using Accounting Data." *Sloan Management Review* 12 (September 1971).

Index

About the Author

Harlan D. Platt is an assistant professor of finance in the College of Business at Northeastern University. In addition to bankruptcy, his research interests include financial markets, stock and index options, and energy. His publications have appeared in the *Energy Journal, Business Horizons, Akron Business and Economics Review,* and the *Journal of Financial Education,* among others. Prior to joining Northeastern's faculty in 1981, he was the director of electricity research and forecasting at Data Resources, Inc. His accomplishments there included authoring three books on electricity demand forecasting. He received his Ph.D. in economics from the University of Michigan and earned his B.A. degree from Northwestern University.